Glencoe
Entrepreneurship
Building a Business

Web-Based Businesses
Academic Integration
Project-Based Learning

In Partnership with
**STANDARD
&POOR'S**

Student Activity Workbook
with Academic Integration

Glencoe

Send all inquiries to:
4400 Easton Commons
Columbus, OH 43219

ISBN: 978-0-07-894325-6   (Student Activity Workbook)
MHID: 0-07-894325-6   (Student Activity Workbook)

4 5 6 7 8 9   QVS   18 17 16 15 14

Table of Contents

Table of Contents

Table of Contents

Table of Contents

Name _____ Date _____ Class _____

Chapter 1 What Is Entrepreneurship?

 Note Taking

Directions As you read, write notes, facts, and main ideas in the note-taking column. Write key words and short phrases in the cues column. Then summarize the section in the summary box.

Cues	Note Taking
• entrepreneur and entrepreneurship	**ENTREPRENEURSHIP AND THE ECONOMY** • Entrepreneurs undertake the creation, organization, and ownership of a business, as well as the risks of a venture.
• entrepreneurship became popular in 1980s	**THE ENTREPRENEURIAL PROCESS** • Large diversified companies with no competition were common in the U.S. in the 1960s, but economic changes increased entrepreneurship's importance over the decades.
Summary	

Chapter 1 *What Is Entrepreneurship?* 1

Chapter 1

Chapter 1 What Is Entrepreneurship?
Section 1.1 Entrepreneurship and the Economy
Section Review: Critical Thinking

Directions Entrepreneurs help shape the economy and have an impact on our social and cultural development. In this activity, you will identify some of today's entrepreneurs. You will also develop your own definition of an entrepreneur and examine how such people affect your life. Answer the questions.

1. Based on your reading and experience, what is your definition of an entrepreneur?

   _____

   _____

   _____

2. Identify three modern entrepreneurs and the nature of their business activity. These can be persons from your community or persons you have heard or read about elsewhere. You may use library resources or the Internet to help identify these persons.

   _____

   _____

   _____

   _____

3. Explain your reason(s) for choosing these three entrepreneurs. In your answer, be sure to describe how they are examples of your definition of an entrepreneur.

   _____

   _____

   _____

4. What impact do you think these entrepreneurs have on the economy and current business climate? Is it positive or negative? Explain.

   _____

   _____

   _____

   _____

Chapter 1 What Is Entrepreneurship?

Section 1.2 The Entrepreneurial Process

Section Review: Analysis

Directions You are going to open a pizza delivery business where no eat-in service will be provided. Your clients will be able to call in an order for quickly made pizza that can be delivered or picked up to go.

Before you begin, you must identify the factors of production required to operate such a business. (Remember that these are resources used by a business.) Using the four factors discussed in the chapter as organizational categories, brainstorm and identify all the needed items. *Hint:* Do research on the Internet or interview the owner of a pizza delivery business if you need help.

1. **Land/Natural Resources**

   _____

   _____

   _____

2. **Labor**

   _____

   _____

   _____

3. **Capital**

   _____

   _____

   _____

4. **Entrepreneurship**

   _____

   _____

   _____

Chapter 1 What Is Entrepreneurship?

Software Activity
Spreadsheet Application

Directions As you consider opportunities in starting a new business, you might want to look into franchising possibilities. Many entrepreneurs feel franchises offer them many advantages. They are opening a business based on a proven formula and have the benefit of a parent company that will be able to provide suggestions and assistance when needed. At the same time, the entrepreneur is still his or her own boss.

The objective of this activity is to identify franchises with growth potential.

Practice Situation You have researched various franchise opportunities and want to see which category has the highest growth potential. How do you go about such an investigation?

On the printout below is a record of current sales for various types of franchises. The estimated sales for these areas in the next five years are also recorded. Calculate the expected growth rate for each franchise category by dividing the difference in sales by the current sales.

SELECTED FRANCHISE INDUSTRIES (SALES IN MILLIONS)

Business Category	Current Sales	Anticipated Sales in 5 Years	Growth (%)
Food and Restaurant	$56,538	$97,234	
Retailing (Nonfood)	$31,468	$55,221	
Hotels/Motels	$22,075	$30,647	
Health and Senior Care	$21,954	$50,712	
Business Services	$16,371	$31,605	
Automotive Products and Services	$13,410	$19,452	
Property Maintenance	$11,982	$14,359	
Rental Services	$10,115	$16,450	
Construction and Home Services	$7,640	$10,020	
Recreation/ Entertainment/Travel	$3,256	$5,109	

Spreadsheet Directions

1. Start your spreadsheet software program.

2. Re-create the table from the previous page using your spreadsheet program.

3. Enter a formula to calculate anticipated growth rate for each of the franchise categories.

4. After completing your calculations, save your work.

5. Print out a copy of your work if your teacher has instructed you to do so.

Interpreting Results

1. Provide examples of specific businesses that fall under each of the categories listed. Use library or Internet resources if needed.

   _____

   _____

   _____

   _____

2. Which franchise category has the fastest anticipated growth rate?

   _____

   _____

3. Which franchise category has the slowest anticipated growth rate?

   _____

   _____

Drawing Conclusions

4. Why do many potential entrepreneurs consider a slow anticipated growth rate as a reason not to consider a business opportunity?

   _____

   _____

   _____

   _____

Chapter 1 What Is Entrepreneurship?

Academic Integration Activity

 English Language Arts
Reading Skills

Directions Match each content vocabulary word or term to its definition. Write the word or term on the line next to its definition.

- scarcity
- equilibrium
- Gross Domestic Product
- entrepreneurship
- venture
- goods
- services
- need

- want
- entrepreneur
- economics
- free enterprise system
- profit
- market structure
- supply
- business cycle

- monopoly
- oligopoly
- factors of production
- demand
- elastic demand
- inelastic demand
- diminishing marginal utility

1. _____ Nature and degree of competition among businesses operating in same industry

2. _____ Amount of goods or services that producers are willing to provide

3. _____ Individual who undertakes the creation, organization, and ownership of a business

4. _____ Physical products that satisfy consumers' wants or needs

5. _____ Money left over after all expenses of running a business have been deducted from the income

6. _____ Point at which consumers buy all of a product that is supplied

7. _____ Quantity of goods or services that consumers are willing and able to buy at various places

8. _____ Difference between demand and supply

9. _____ Economic system found in most democratic nations

10. _____ A basic requirement for survival

11. _____ Nonphysical products that satisfy consumers' wants and needs

12. _____ Process of recognizing and testing an opportunity and gathering resources necessary to go into business

13. _____ A new business undertaking that involves risk

14. _____ Study of how people allocate scarce resources to fulfill their unlimited wants

15. _____ General pattern of an economy's expansion and contraction

16. _____ Effect or law that establishes that price alone does not determine demand

17. _____ Resources businesses use to produce goods and services

18. _____ Situations in which a change in price has little or no effect on demand

19. _____ Market structure in which a particular commodity has only one seller

20. _____ Situations in which a change in prices creates a change in demand

21. _____ Market structure in which there are just a few competing firms

22. _____ The total market value of all goods and services produced within a nation during a given period

23. _____ Something that you do not have to have for survival, but would like to have

Chapter 1 What Is Entrepreneurship?

Academic Integration Activity

 Social Studies
Global Business

Directions All over the globe, entrepreneurs try to identify people's needs and wants. Write the letter of a good or service on the line next to the number of the person who would most need or want it.

Goods or Services

a. French-speaking tour guide

b. heavy protective gloves

c. wetsuit

d. espresso machine

e. athletic shoes

f. Spanish-English dictionary

g. rope clips

h. irrigation consultant

i. buttons

j. egg incubator

Who Needs or Wants It?

_____ **1.** A mountain climbing guide in Nepal

_____ **2.** A British student attending language school in Guatemala

_____ **3.** A farming collective in Uganda

_____ **4.** An ostrich breeder in Iran

_____ **5.** A coffee barista in Colombia

_____ **6.** A textile factory owner in Sri Lanka

_____ **7.** A tourist visiting Versailles

_____ **8.** A long-distance runner training in Kenya

_____ **9.** A surfer in Hawaii

_____ **10.** An ice delivery person in Japan

Directions List the main attributes of each market structure, then answer the question. Some attributes are listed for you.

Perfect Competition
Industry has numerous buyers and sellers.

Monopolistic Competition
Many sellers produce similar but differentiated results.

Monopoly
One seller has control over supply and near total control over prices.

Oligopoly
Industry has a few competing firms.

1. Explain reasons why competition is beneficial to consumers.

_____

_____

_____

_____

_____

_____

_____

_____

_____

_____

_____

_____

_____

_____

Chapter 1 What Is Entrepreneurship?
Case Study Activity
Entrepreneurial Success

Directions Read the *BusinessWeek* Case Study in this chapter. Then read this case study and answer the questions.

CISCO PUSHES FURTHER INTO CONSUMER TERRITORY
By Stephen H. Wildstrom

In a recession, the strong get stronger, and the small or weak get eaten. Cisco Systems, the San Jose, Calif., maker of networking gear, announced it was snapping up Pure Digital Technologies, maker of the wildly popular Flip line of inexpensive video cameras, for $590 million in stock. Coming on the heels of Cisco's announcement that it was moving into the server business, the acquisition is another sign that Cisco is pushing aggressively into new markets at a time when many of its competitors are hobbled.

The Flip cameras arguably will be the first true consumer products under the Cisco umbrella, but the company has been sidling into consumer markets for a while now. Evidence shows that Cisco wants to expand the market from technical components such as wireless routers that no one wants to see or think about into true consumer electronics. Adding Pure Digital to this mix of products begins to make sense. The Flip video cameras, starting at about $150, are ridiculously easy to use, produce surprisingly good images, and offer simple uploads to services such as YouTube and Flickr. And they move the Cisco line into the fast-expanding area of content creation.

Catering to homes complements Cisco's other businesses, too. Communications providers need switches and routers to handle all that network traffic generated by video uploads and shared film clips. "Pure Digital will add to Cisco's arsenal of products aimed at driving increased network bandwidth, similar to Cisco's videoconferencing products," UBS analysts write in a March 19 research note. "As more consumers upload video content to the Web, it will also drive demand for Cisco's traditional products—switches and routers."

If there's a piece missing from the puzzle, it's a simple way to get the video onto a TV set instead of a computer.

(Excerpted from *BusinessWeek.com*, March 19, 2009)

1. What happened to Pure Digital Technologies in March 2009?

_____

_____

2. Write two reasons why the Flip camera was popular during hard economic times.

_____

_____

_____

3. Why did Cisco purchase Pure Digital?

_____

_____

_____

4. Describe how Pure Digital succeeded as a business.

_____

_____

_____

5. According to the article, what is a consumer want that still needs to be fulfilled?

_____

_____

_____

6. Write 1, 2, and 3 to show the order of events.

_____ Cisco buys Pure Digital Technologies.

_____ Pure Digital Technologies makes the Flip line of video cameras.

_____ Cisco announces a move into the server business.

Chapter 1 What Is Entrepreneurship?

Interpreting Information

Test Taking

Directions Some charts you find on tests look simple but contain a lot of information. The chart below shows the age groups and educational degrees of founders of U.S. technology startup companies. Study the chart and fill in the bubble next to the best answer to each question. Use only the information that has been provided in the chart to help you choose your answer.

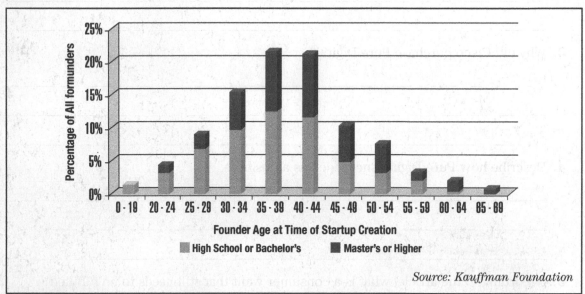

Source: Kauffman Foundation

1. According to this chart, the highest percentage of U.S. technology startup company founders comes from which age group?
   - ○ 30–34
   - ○ 35–39
   - ○ 40–44
   - ○ 45–49

2. Which age group has the lowest percentage of postgraduate degrees (PhD, MD, JD)?
   - ○ 0–19
   - ○ 30–34
   - ○ 50–54
   - ○ 65–69

3. Approximately what percentage of all tech founders were between 35 and 39 years old and had attained up to a bachelor's degree at the time of startup?
   - ○ 1%
   - ○ 6%
   - ○ 10%
   - ○ 22%

4. Approximately what percentage of all tech startup founders had attained a postgraduate (Master's or higher) degree?
   - ○ 15%
   - ○ 25%
   - ○ 45%
   - ○ 60%

5. Which age group had the highest percentage of founders who had some college experience, but no bachelor's or postgraduate degree?
   - ○ 0–19
   - ○ 30–34
   - ○ 55–59
   - ○ information not given in graph

Chapter 2 Your Potential as an Entrepreneur

 Note Taking

Directions As you read, write notes, facts, and main ideas in the note-taking column. Write key words and short phrases in the cues column. Then summarize the section in the summary box.

Cues	Note Taking
	WHY BE AN ENTREPRENEUR?
• greatest rewards of entrepreneurship are intangible	• Entrepreneurs enjoy being own boss, doing something they enjoy, being creative, setting own schedule, and having opportunity to control destiny and make more money.
• entrepreneurs are subjects of great interest worldwide	**WHAT DOES IT TAKE TO BE AN ENTREPRENEUR?** • Research has been done to figure out the common traits, experiences, and skills of entrepreneurs.
Summary	

Chapter 2

Chapter 2 Your Potential as an Entrepreneur

Section 2.1 Why Be an Entrepreneur?

Section Review: Apply

Directions Developing your entrepreneurial potential is often as simple as looking inside yourself. Using the categories mentioned below as a guide, list as many entrepreneurial experiences as you can from your everyday life. A few examples are provided to help you get started.

School
- Creating posters and Web pages for school events
- Making oral presentations in class

_____

_____

Family/Home
- Balancing a budget
- Shopping around for best prices

_____

_____

Jobs
- Taking responsibility for important tasks
- Interacting with customers

_____

_____

Hobbies/Interests
- Choosing what to do with your free time
- Joining local special interest clubs

_____

_____

Traveling
- Learning about other cultures
- Overcoming communication barriers

_____

_____

Chapter 2 Your Potential as an Entrepreneur

Section 2.2 What Does It Take to Be an Entrepreneur?

Section Review: Critical Thinking

Directions Do you possess any of the distinctive traits that are commonly shared by entrepreneurs? This two-part exercise will help you examine your own potential to become an entrepreneur. It will also help you think about ways to develop and refine these characteristics.

A. Listed below are the characteristics or distinctive traits of a successful entrepreneur. Rank yourself for each of the traits listed. Decide if each trait is most like you (5) or least like you (1). If you fall somewhere in between, circle the number that you feel is the best indicator.

Characteristic	Most Like Me				Least Like Me
1. Persistent	5	4	3	2	1
2. Creative	5	4	3	2	1
3. Responsible	5	4	3	2	1
4. Realistic	5	4	3	2	1
5. Goal-oriented	5	4	3	2	1
6. Independent	5	4	3	2	1
7. Self-demanding	5	4	3	2	1
8. Self-confident	5	4	3	2	1
9. Risk-taking	5	4	3	2	1
10. Restless	5	4	3	2	1
11. Action-oriented	5	4	3	2	1
12. Enthusiastic	5	4	3	2	1

Continued on next page

Chapter 2

B. This part of the exercise will help you identify areas where you might want to seek more experiences. Consider the way you rated yourself on the previous page. As you do, answer the following questions about your entrepreneurial potential.

1. What have you learned about yourself from filling out the chart on the previous page?

_____

_____

_____

_____

2. Which areas are your strengths?

_____

_____

_____

_____

3. In which areas could you improve?

_____

_____

_____

_____

4. For each category in which you ranked yourself 3 or lower, identify experiences, activities, and ways in which you could improve your entrepreneurial potential.

_____

_____

_____

_____

_____

_____

_____

_____

_____

_____

Chapter 2 Your Potential as an Entrepreneur
Case Study Activity
Young Entrepreneurs

Directions Read the *BusinessWeek* Case Study in this chapter and complete the following activity.

Each year *BusinessWeek* magazine selects finalists for America's best young entrepreneurs age 25 and younger. In a recent year, nine of the 25 finalist companies were minority-run businesses. Use library resources and the Internet, including BusinessWeek.com, to complete the chart below. The first one is completed for you. Then pick one company other than Eden Body Works for additional research. Use the information you learn to answer the questions on the next page.

Name(s)	Company	Function of Company
Jasmine Lawrence	Eden Body Works	Natural hair-care products
Anik Singal	Affiliate Classroom (affiliate classroom.com)	
Carlos Leon	CML Studios (cmlstudios.net)	
Daniel Negari	Beverly Hills Mint (beverlyhillsmint.com)	
Ibtihaj Amatul-Wahad	Ippy's Islamic Fashions (no Web site)	
Artia Moghbel	SchoolRack (schoolrack.com)	
Ebele Mora, Jason Smikle, Fabrizio Sousa	Truly Unique Vision (tuvcollegemarketing.com)	
Brandon Davenport, Elwood Green III, Marcellus Alexander	Vesta Mobile Solutions (vestamobile.com)	

Continued on next page

Answer the following questions about the company you selected.

1. Where is the company located?

   _____

   _____

   _____

   _____

2. What is the background of your entrepreneur(s)? These could be things such as interests, hobbies, education, and previous work experience.

   _____

   _____

   _____

   _____

   _____

3. From what you have read about the company, describe a hypothetical situation in which a customer purchases the company's goods or services. What does the customer want? How is the good or service delivered? How much might the customer pay?

   _____

   _____

   _____

   _____

   _____

4. Look at the list of 12 entrepreneurial characteristics on pages 38 and 39 of your book. From what you have read about your entrepreneur(s), how many of these characteristics describe this person or people? Explain why.

   _____

   _____

   _____

   _____

   _____

Name _____ Date _____ Class _____

Chapter 2 Your Potential as an Entrepreneur
Academic Integration Activity

 **Mathematics**
Reading Tables

Directions The table provides details about small businesses in the United States by number of establishments, number of paid employees, and annual payroll in a recent year. Study the table and answer the questions.

EMPLOYMENT SIZE OF ENTERPRISE

Number of Employees	Number of Establishments	Number of Paid Employees	Annual Payroll
1 to 4	2,782,252	5,844,637	$165,904,564
5 to 9	1,055,937	6,852,769	$195,519,100
10 to 19	666,574	8,499,681	$257,802,789
20 to 99	692,697	20,642,614	$670,418,442
100 to 499	330,447	16,757,751	$587,676,161
500 or more	1,056,482	56,477,472	$2,336,631,127
10,000 or more	587,168	30,438,785	$1,266,117,990

Information obtained from *http://www.census.gov/epcd/www/smallbus.html*

1. What is the total number of establishments that have 100 to 499 employees in the United States?

_____

2. What is the annual payroll for establishments that have 5 to 9 employees?

3. How many paid employees are part of the group with the smallest number of establishments?

_____

4. How many paid employees are part of the group with the highest number of establishments?

_____

5. Which group of employees has the highest annual payroll?

_____

6. How many paid employees work for establishments that employ 10,000 or more people?

_____

7. Based on the information in the table, how many employees work for establishments that have 500 to 9,999 employees?

_____

Chapter 2 Your Potential as an Entrepreneur
Academic Integration Activity
 Social Studies
Entrepreneurial Characteristics

Directions The following cases illustrate how enterpreneurial characteristics come into play in day-to-day activities. Read each case and answer the related questions.

Case 1

Chaz has an idea for a service business. It has worked well in other markets, and Chaz sees no reason why it should not work locally. The service involves renting DVDs about colleges and universities to high school students. The colleges Chaz has contacted are all for it, and the students he has talked to are excited about the idea as well. However, the three banks from which he has tried to borrow money to set up his business are skeptical. They have all turned him down for a loan.

What entrepreneurial characteristic should kick in here if Chaz's business is going to become a reality? Why is that characteristic so important in this situation? Why is it important to entrepreneurs in general?

_____

_____

_____

_____

Case 2

Sonia has often thought of going into business for herself. She has had a lot of great ideas. They must have been great, she thinks, because other people have made a lot of money with similar concepts. Sonia just never seems to get started on putting her ideas to work.

What should Sonia do if she wants to turn her ideas into reality? What entrepreneurial characteristic does she need to develop? Why is it important to all entrepreneurs?

_____

_____

_____

_____

Case 3

Will has been working overtime and weekends for almost two years. He wants to save up enough money so he can open his own electrical repair shop. Today, something happened that could be a big break for him. His employer offered to finance 60% of Will's venture for 51% ownership. Will is reluctant. It would mean that he could get his venture underway almost immediately. But it would also mean that he would be giving up control of the business.

What entrepreneurial characteristic is evident in Will's reluctance? Why is that characteristic so important to entrepreneurs? What should he do?

_____

_____

_____

_____

Case 4

Several food service operations have gone in and out of business in Elliot's town in the last few years. Despite this, Elliot strongly believes he can be successful in that type of business. He is convinced that a health-conscious menu, extra good service, and promotion targeting people who are concerned about nutrition will be a winning combination. His family, friends, and even some people who have been in the restaurant business are trying to talk Elliot out of his idea, but he is convinced it can work.

What entrepreneurial characteristic is in operation here? Why is it important to the success of entrepreneurs? What do you think of his chances of success? Why?

_____

_____

_____

_____

Case 5

A few years ago, Kami started a rental management company. Recently, however, she decided to expand her business by buying some apartment buildings of her own. Right now she is looking at three properties. One is a fourplex. All units in this property have been rented for years, but have a very low profit yield. The second, a five-unit building, has not had a good rental history. It could, however, double in value if it and adjacent properties can be sold to a commercial-property developer. The chance of this happening is about one in 50. The third property, which has six apartments, also has a poor rental history. With some remodeling and a management change, though, it should produce a solid return.

Which property do you think Kami should buy? Why? What entrepreneurial characteristic would be an important factor in her decision? Why is this characteristic important to the success of entrepreneurs?

_____

_____

_____

_____

Chapter 2 Your Potential as an Entrepreneur

Software Activity
PowerPoint Application

Directions The objective of this activity is to identify the characteristics and traits of an entrepreneur.

Before starting a business, potential entrepreneurs should consider the characteristics and skills that will help them succeed. One way to do that is to study the profile of successful entrepreneurs. These examples are all around you. They are featured in reports in magazines and on the Internet. Entrepreneurs can even be found in your own neighborhood.

Choose a successful entrepreneur you would like to learn more about. Through library research, the Internet, or a personal interview, identify the following:

- the characteristics and skills this entrepreneur possesses
- his/her background
- distinctive traits and qualities he/she possesses that caused him/her to be successful as an entrepreneur
- skills the entrepreneur possesses that were essential to establishing a business

Next, develop a slide presentation that describes the background, characteristics, and skills of the entrepreneur you have selected. Use several different types of slides (as shown in the printout below) to present your findings. One should be a title slide and at least one of the slides should include clipart.

Entrepreneur's Name

Entrepreneur's Background
- **College graduate**
- **Technical training**
- **4 years of work experience**

Entrepreneur's Characteristics
- **Persistent**
- **Creative**

PowerPoint Directions

1. Start your PowerPoint software program.

2. Based on the information you have collected about the entrepreneur, develop a minimum of six slides that will describe the background, characteristics, and skills of this entrepreneur.

3. Print out a copy of your slides if your teacher has instructed you to do so.

4. Answer the following questions.

Interpreting Results

1. Why is it important for entrepreneurs to have role models?

_____

_____

_____

_____

_____

2. Present your slide presentation to your class. What characteristics and skills were common to all the entrepreneurs presented? List any characteristics and skills that were distinctive to one of the entrepreneurs.

_____

_____

_____

_____

_____

Drawing Conclusions

3. Why is it important for potential entrepreneurs to identify the background, characteristics, and skills of successful entrepreneurs?

_____

_____

_____

_____

_____

Chapter 2 Your Potential as an Entrepreneur

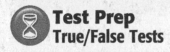 **Test Prep**
True/False Tests

Directions Read the following tips on taking true/false tests, then take the practice test below. Circle *T* for true or *F* for false. Rewrite false statements so that they are true.

TAKING TRUE/FALSE TESTS
• Answer *true* only when every part of a statement is true. If part of the statement is false, the entire statement is false.
• Watch out for words such as *always*, *never*, *every*, or *none*. These usually indicate a false answer. Most statements are not always or never true.
• Statements with words such as *usually*, *sometimes*, or *often* are usually true statements.

1. Entrepreneurs try to emulate the attitudes and achievements of a role model.   **T   F**

_____

2. Achievers tend to become discouraged by difficulties.   **T   F**

_____

3. Employees risk losing money invested in a business.   **T   F**

_____

4. Buildings, equipment, tools, and other goods are considered capital.   **T   F**

_____

5. Entrepreneurs blame others if their decisions turn out to be wrong.   **T   F**

_____

6. Competition is a significant challenge in starting a business.   **T   F**

_____

Chapter 3 Recognizing Opportunity

 Note Taking

Directions As you read, write notes, facts, and main ideas in the note-taking column. Write key words and short phrases in the cues column. Then summarize the section in the summary box.

Cues	Note Taking
• entrepreneurial process	**UNDERSTANDING ENTREPRENEURIAL TRENDS** • To begin the entrepreneurial process: 1. recognize opportunity; 2. develop a business concept; 3. test it with potential customers; 4. create business to execute concept.
• values	**STARTING VERSUS BUYING A BUSINESS** • When considering whether to go into business it is helpful to consider your values, the beliefs and principles you live by, and use them to help guide your pursuits and set your objectives.

Summary

Chapter 3 Recognizing Opportunity

Section 3.1 Understanding Entrepreneurial Trends

Section Review: Apply

Directions Find three small boxes or containers. In the first container, place 12 small pieces of paper, each containing a word for a flavor. In the second container, place 12 small pieces of paper, each containing a word for a color. In the third container, place 12 small pieces of paper, each containing a word or words for an animal or a place. Now without looking, pull one piece of paper from each container. List the words on the three spaces below.

1. _____

2. _____

3. _____

Now see if you can create a new product or service by using at least two of the three words. If, after several attempts, you want to try again, choose another set of words. Be sure to record your ideas in the space below. You may be surprised at the interesting ideas you can come up with if you let your mind think freely.

_____

_____

_____

_____

_____

_____

_____

_____

_____

_____

_____

_____

_____

_____

_____

Chapter 3 Recognizing Opportunity

Section 3.2 Starting Versus Buying a Business

Section Review: Critical Thinking

Directions Entrepreneurs in all areas of business are faced with numerous decisions every day. In many cases, their success depends on how well they examine a situation and make a decision. Your success with this activity will depend on how well you analyze the information given below, using the steps in the formal decision-making process.

Situation You are the owner of a local flower shop. Two of your business associates are having weddings on Saturday, and you have been hired to design the floral arrangements for both weddings. The plans have been finalized for months, and the two couples are expecting perfect weddings. Orders for some of the flowers were placed weeks ago because several of the flowers being used are grown only in tropical climates and are difficult to obtain.

It is the Monday before the weddings. On the previous Thursday, a hurricane ripped through the Hawaiian Islands. Your major suppliers of flowers are located on the islands, and you have just received a text message that the current crop of flowers has been destroyed. What might be salvaged is not available for immediate shipment because the airports will be closed for several days. The earliest that you might receive a shipment would be Friday, the day before the weddings.

Your challenge, if you want to maintain the good opinion of your associates and continue in business, is to solve this problem using the steps in formal decision making as outlined below. Try to be creative and realistic as you come up with a solution (or solutions) to address this difficult situation. Space is provided on this and the next page for you to work through your decision.

You may need additional sheets of paper to explore your ideas thoroughly. Be entrepreneurial as you come up with your solution.

1. Identify the problem or opportunity. Based on the information given, state the problem or opportunity as you see it.

   _____

   _____

   _____

2. List the solutions or options. Explain as many possible solutions as you can. (Consider contacting a florist if you need help.)

   _____

   _____

   _____

Continued on next page

Chapter 3

3. Evaluate the alternatives. Discuss each alternative, weighing its advantages and disadvantages.

_____

_____

_____

_____

_____

_____

4. Choose a solution. Explain the reasons for your choice.

_____

_____

_____

_____

_____

_____

5. Act and get feedback. What will you do to carry out your plan to solve the problem? How will you know if you are successful?

_____

_____

_____

_____

_____

_____

_____

_____

_____

Chapter 3

Chapter 3 Recognizing Opportunity

Case Study Activity

Starting a Company

Directions Read the *BusinessWeek* Case Study feature in this chapter of your textbook. Then read the information below and complete the Case Study Activity.

TESLA ALUM TAKES ON BATTERY TECH AT STARTUP ATIEVA
By Josie Garthwaite

The team at battery tech startup Atieva did not plan on using electric-car maker Tesla Motors as Battery Class 101. But many of the engineers at the two-year-old startup and almost a third of the founding team learned the ropes at Tesla before joining Atieva. Founded by former Tesla Vice-President Bernard Tse and Astoria Networks founder Sam Weng, the company is developing software for monitoring individual battery cells, mechanical packaging, and controls for battery packs in plug-in vehicles.

Atieva is not using the technology worked on at Tesla, but Mike Harrigan, another former Tesla VP who joined Atieva earlier this year, said in an interview that the new venture still takes lessons from Tesla. In addition to the industry connections Tse made during his time there, he and other engineers acquired basic knowledge about the demands on electric-car batteries. Such expertise may help Atieva to avoid some of the delays, detours, and financial troubles that Tesla has encountered.

Tesla Motors initially planned to enter a similar business—battery tech supply— through a division called the Tesla Energy Group. According to a 2007 blog post by Tesla founder Martin Eberhard on the official Tesla blog, it was "impossible to hire people with 'prior experience.'" The electric-car battery tech sector was simply too new for many people to have any significant experience in it. Tse moved on after Tesla shifted gears to focus on its main product, the Tesla Roadster, and started Atieva in 2007.

Harrigan said Atieva plans to design custom vehicle battery packs for each customer, and aims to work with whatever cells an automaker wants to use or that a cell-maker wants packaged. Right now, Atieva is working with China's Lishen to build 3,000 battery packs for buses in China as part of a nationally subsidized initiative. Harrigan said Atieva is also "in active talks" with Chinese and European automakers that are interested in deploying test fleets of electric vehicles, as well as a U.S.-based electric motorcycle maker. Ultimately, Atieva aims to be something like a Magna International or Bosch—auto parts suppliers—for smaller, independent plug-in carmakers.

Tesla, meanwhile, has revived its battery division, and recently snagged a battery pack supply deal with automaker Daimler. It hopes to get funds to set up manufacturing for its planned Model S sedan. So for now, for both companies, it is wait and see.

Excerpted from *BusinessWeek* May 28, 2009

Continued on next page

Chapter 3

1. What does Atieva provide to its customers?

_____

_____

_____

2. At this time, what kind of market is the electric-car market?

_____

_____

_____

3. What similarities does Atieva have to Tesla Motors? How is Atieva different from Tesla?

_____

_____

_____

_____

4. Why did Tesla initially have trouble producing its own battery packs?

_____

_____

_____

_____

5. Which company has outsourced production work to Atieva? Describe the deal between the two companies.

_____

_____

_____

_____

6. Give an example from the article of how Tesla is attempting to become Atieva's competitor.

_____

_____

_____

_____

_____

Chapter 3 Recognizing Opportunity

Academic Integration Activity

 English Language Arts
Writing Skills

Directions Write a paragraph that correctly uses 10 or more of the content vocabulary terms listed in this chapter of your text book. The paragraph might be about an idea you have, or about an entrepreneur's efforts to start a business. Be creative!

_____

_____

_____

_____

_____

_____

_____

_____

_____

_____

_____

_____

_____

_____

_____

_____

_____

_____

_____

_____

_____

_____

_____

_____

_____

_____

Chapter 3

Chapter 3 Recognizing Opportunity
Academic Integration Activity

Science
Biotechnology

Directions Read the article describing biotechnology and the "History of Biotechnology" time line. Then answer the questions.

WHAT IS BIOTECHNOLOGY?

The definition of biotechnology varies, but a simple definition is the use of organisms by humans. One example of biotechnology is cloning. We have been cloning plants for centuries. Each time a leaf is excised from a violet plant and placed in soil to grow a new plant, cloning has occurred. Today, we are not only doing the physical manipulation at the visual level but also on the molecular level. In modern or molecular biotechnology, we physically select the desired characteristic at the molecular level and add it to the organism's genetic makeup.

Biotechnology is the science for this century. Humans have expanded their understanding of the biosphere by journeying into space and exploring the depths of the ocean. The advancement of tools and techniques is now allowing us to look at the universe of atoms. Biotechnology is utilizing the sciences of biology, chemistry, physics, engineering, computers, and information technology to develop tools and products that hold great promise and concern. Humans have always been "manipulating" organisms to their advantage, but now we are able to manipulate life and materials at the atomic level through nanotechnology.

The two schools of thought about what biotechnology is can elicit much debate. Both use organisms to help man. Whereas modern biotechnology manipulates the genes of organisms and inserts them into other organisms to acquire the desired trait, traditional biotechnology uses the processes of organisms, such as fermentation.

Source: www.biotechinsitute.org

1. What is the simple definition of biotechnology?

_____

_____

2. What is the main difference between the old method of cloning plants described in the article and the modern method?

_____

_____

_____

3. Name the technology that allows humans to manipulate materials at the atomic level.

_____

HISTORY OF BIOTECHNOLOGY

BC

1750 • The Sumerians brew beer.

500 • The Chinese use moldy soybean curds to treat boils.

100 • Powdered chrysanthemum is used in China as an insecticide.

AD

1590 • The microscope is invented by Hans and Zaccharaias Janssen.

1663 • Cells are first described by Robert Hooke.

1797 • Edward Jenner inoculates a child with a viral vaccine to keep him from smallpox.

1855 • The *Escherichia coli* bacterium is discovered. It later becomes a major research, development, and production tool for biotechnology.

1879 • Walther Flemming discovers chromatin, the rod-like structures inside the cell nucleus that later come to be called "chromosomes."

1883 • The first rabies vaccine is developed.

1906 • The term "genetics" is introduced.

1909 • Genes are linked with hereditary disorders.

1914 • Bacteria are used to treat sewage for the first time in Manchester, England.

1919 • The word "biotechnology" is first used by a Hungarian agricultural engineer.

1928 • Alexander Fleming discovers penicillin, the first antibiotic.

1943 • Oswald T. Avery demonstrates that DNA is the material of genes.

1953 • James D. Watson and Francis Crick reveal the three-dimensional structure of DNA.

1961 • The genetic code is understood for the first time.

1972 • The DNA composition of humans is discovered to be 99% similar to that of chimpanzees and gorillas.

1977 • Genetically engineered bacteria are used to synthesize human growth protein.

1981 • The first genetically engineered plant is reported; mice are successfully cloned.

1984 • The DNA fingerprinting technique is developed

1988 • Congress funds the Human Genome Project, a massive effort to map and sequence the human genetic code as well as the genomes of other species.

1989 • Microorganisms are used to clean up the Exxon Valdez oil spill; the gene responsible for cystic fibrosis is discovered.

1998 • Human skin is produced in vitro.

1999 • The complete genetic code of the human chromosome is first deciphered.

2003 • Dolly, the cloned sheep that made headlines in 1997, is euthanized after developing progressive lung disease. Dolly was the first successful clone of a mammal.

Continued on next page

Chapter 3

5. What happened first, the use of organisms to treat sores or the use of dried plants to kill insects?

_____

6. What earlier event made it possible for Robert Hooke to see and describe cells?

_____

7. In what years on the timeline were vaccines or antibiotics developed?

_____

8. Since what year has the word "genetics" been a scientific term?

_____

9. In what year was the word "biotechnology" first used?

_____

10. Who first established that DNA is the material of genes? How many years later was DNA's structure revealed?

_____

11. How many years passed between the first cloning of mice and the first cloned sheep?

_____

12. Which environmental disaster cleanup was aided by microorganisms?

_____

13. Since what year has the genetic code been understood?

_____

14. Which of the events on the timeline was important for crimefighting?

_____

Chapter 3

Chapter 3 Recognizing Opportunity
Academic Integration Activity

Software Activity
Internet Research Tools

Directions The objective of this activity is to use Google News Timeline to research current articles about sustainability.

Google News Timeline is an innovative, versatile way for Internet users to instantly find up-to-date and historical news stories about any subject. Once you learn how to use it, it can be a valuable research tool, whether you are a student writing a report or an aspiring entrepreneur looking for a business idea. The site accesses the archives of newspapers and magazines in addition to Web sites. By adding time to your search query, you can actually read history in the making.

Internet Research Directions

1. Open your Web browser and use the search engine to find Google News Timeline.

2. Go to Google News Timeline.

3. In the search engine next to the "News" drop-down menu, type "environment sustainability."

4. Expand sources by clicking on "Add More Queries." Click on boxes to add available newspapers, magazines, and blogs. Click "Save changes" or "Cancel add queries" to return to the main page.

5. Use "Show" drop-down menu to show stories from the current day, week, month, or year. Clicking on "decade" will return older search items.

6. Scroll down to see all stories for the period of time you specify.

7. Use "Size" drop-down menu to change column size.

8. Use site functions to research and answer the following questions.

Interpreting Results

1. Select the three most recent stories published about environmental sustainability. Then provide the following information.

Date and time _____

Source _____

Article title _____

Main Idea _____

_____

_____

_____

Continued on next page

Date and time _____

Source _____

Article title _____

Main Idea _____

_____

_____

_____

Date and time _____

Source _____

Article title _____

Main Idea _____

_____

_____

_____

2. Using the "Decade" search function, what was the oldest article you found about environmental sustainability? Name the source and title, then briefly summarize what you read.

_____

_____

_____

Drawing Conclusions

3. Did you find the search returns to be accurate? Were the stories about sustainability? Explain.

_____

_____

_____

4. Based on what you have learned in this activity, do you think you would use Google News Timeline for future projects? Why or why not? How else might you use this application?

_____

_____

_____

Chapter 3 Recognizing Opportunity

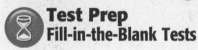

Test Prep
Fill-in-the-Blank Tests

Directions Read these test-taking tips for answering fill-in-the-blank questions. Then use the text to answer the practice-test questions below.

ANSWERING FILL-IN-THE-BLANK QUESTIONS
• Read each question carefully to be sure you understand what is being asked.
• Look for context clues in the question.
• Check to see if the word before the blank is *a* or *an*. If the word is *an*, the answer begins with a vowel.
• Keep your answers brief. This usually means limiting them to one or two words

1. Age, income, and ethnic background are some of the _____ entrepreneurs consider when developing products.

2. A _____ targets readers with special interests in a variety of areas.

3. When an entrepreneur agrees to start a new business using the name of a recognized company, he or she is beginning a _____.

4. _____ measure success by the positive impact they make on society.

5. An entrepreneur seeking _____ wants a venture to avoid compromising the ability of future generations to meet their needs.

6. When an entrepreneur focuses on serving a unique or unfilled market, he or she is targeting a _____.

7. An _____ happens when creativity is used to make connections, which in turn helps create new inventions and products.

8. Examples of _____ include hard work, honesty, and responsibility.

9. A _____ buys the planning and management expertise of an existing business from a _____.

10. A potential entrepreneur may _____, thinking freely to come up with ideas.

11. Anyone with an Internet connection can purchase goods or services from an _____.

12. A large company will supply resources to help a new _____ started from within the company.

Chapter 3

Chapter 4 Global Opportunities

 Note Taking

Directions As you read, write notes, facts, and main ideas in the note-taking column.
Write key words and short phrases in the cues column. Then summarize the section in
the summary box.

Cues	Note Taking
• Businesses sell and buy goods and services to and from other countries.	**GLOBAL ENTREPRENEURSHIP** • The interconnected economies of the world's nations make up the global economy.
• interpreter	**WAYS TO ENTER THE GLOBAL MARKET** • Understanding culture, showing respect, and knowing the way other countries conduct business are musts for entrepreneurs.
Summary	

Chapter 4 Global Opportunities
Section 4.1 Global Entrepreneurship
Section Review: Identify

Directions This activity is based on a portion of an actual interview with The Body Shop founder Anita Roddick. To complete the exercise, read aloud the following material and answer questions 1–6 on the next page.

ANITA RODDICK TALKS

"What is The Body Shop?"

"We make and sell our own naturally based products which cleanse, polish, and protect the skin and hair.

"This is The Body Shop in a nutshell. But it is by no means the whole story.

"I started The Body Shop in Brighton, England, in 1976. There are now over 2,400 The Body Shop stores in 61 countries from Norway to New Zealand. We are trading in more than 20 languages, and we are still growing.

"That kind of success always sparks people's curiosity. They want to know how and why. The answer is as simple as the original idea for The Body Shop. It made sense to me to find out what customers wanted, then try and get it for them and sell them as much or as little of it as they felt like buying without all the unnecessary, expensive packaging, and hype that people associate with the cosmetics industry. I thought it was important that my business concern itself not just with skin and hair care preparations but also with the community, the environment, and the big wide world beyond cosmetics.

"I believe that from the very beginning we tapped into a common thread of humanity. Simplicity has a lot of appeal in an increasingly complex world. So does honesty. That is why our customers cut across all boundaries of age, gender, and nationality. What they all have in common is that they want to know the story behind what they buy. And The Body Shop has many stories to tell, because the ideas and the ingredients for our formulations come from such a rich variety of sources—everything from folkloric recipes that have been tried and tested by human beings for thousands of years to tips harvested by our visits to tribal cultures around the globe. I do not think The Body Shop will ever lose the sense of adventure that is attached to the pursuit of knowledge."

Source: The Body Shop promotional literature

Continued on next page

1. What is The Body Shop?

   _____

   _____

   _____

   _____

   _____

2. When and where was The Body Shop founded?

   _____

   _____

3. How many stores has The Body Shop opened worldwide?

   _____

   _____

4. The Body Shop has stores in how many countries?

   _____

   _____

5. What is the source of The Body Shop's ingredients and formulas?

   _____

   _____

   _____

   _____

6. Who are The Body Shop's primary customers?

   _____

   _____

   _____

   _____

Chapter 4 Global Opportunities

Section 4.2 Ways to Enter the Global Market

Section Review: Explain

Directions When meeting with people who speak a different language, you should not always count on body language and gestures to communicate your intended message accurately. Below is a list of gestures that are common in the United States. Read the description of each, and in the second column of the chart briefly explain what it means in this country.

An alternate meaning for another country is also given. Imagine how confusing your message might be in these places if you misused these gestures!

Gesture	Meaning in the United States	Meaning in Other Countries
1. Head and nod		In Bulgaria and Greece, signifies no
2. V sign, palm out		In most of Europe, means victory
3. Circle created by touching thumb and forefinger		In Greece, may create enemies as it is considered impolite. In Southern France, means "zero" or "worthless."
4. Crossed fingers		In Europe, means "protection" or "good luck." In Paraguay, may be offensive.
5. Thumbs up		In Australia, a very rude gesture
6. Circular motion of the finger around the ear		In the Netherlands, if someone gives you this signal, it means you have a phone call.
7. Waving the whole hand back and forth in someone's face		In Greece, a serious insult. The closer to the person's face, the more threatening the gesture is considered.
8. Arms folded across your chest		In Finland, means you are arrogant or proud. In Fiji, shows disrespect.

Chapter 4

Chapter 4 Global Opportunities
Case Study Activity
Laptop Computers

Directions Read the *BusinessWeek* Case Study feature in this chapter of your textbook. Then read the information below and complete the Case Study Activity.

The XO

The computer made for One Laptop per Child, the XO, is commonly called a "netbook," a category of laptop computer. The laptop concept goes back more than 40 years and is an example of the kind of innovative thinking that leads to entrepreneurial success.

In 1968, computers were not designed for personal use. They were so heavy and they used so much power that the possibility of carrying a computer in a backpack or under one arm was beyond most people's imaginations at that time. But Alan Kay, an American computer scientist, *could* imagine such a thing. Kay came up with the idea of the Dynabook, a small computer designed for educational purposes. The Dynabook never became reality, but Kay's early sketches look somewhat like today's laptop computers. Kay's idea was expanded upon as technology improved and computers became smaller. In 1981, the Osborne 1 became the first commercially available portable computer.

Today, the XO used by children all over the world is based on Alan Kay's Dynabook concept. Kay co-designed the XO with One Laptop per Child founder Nicholas Negroponte.

The chart below shows some of the specifications of the **Osborne 1**. Using the Internet, including search engines and the One Laptop per Child Web site, research the newest version of the XO, the **XO-1**. Use the information you find to complete the chart.

Specifications	Osborne 1	XO-1
Weight	24.5 lbs.	
Random-Access Memory (RAM)	64K	
Monitor size	5 inches	
Operating system	CP/M 2.2	
Power source	wall plug	
Retail cost	$1,750 (approximately $4,100 today)	

Chapter 4

Chapter 4 Global Opportunities

Academic Integration Activity

Mathematics
Interpreting Trade Statistics

Directions The chart shows the total annual imports and exports of selected countries in a recent year. Subtract the amount of imports from the amount of exports to determine the trade balance of each country (this might produce a negative number). Then answer the questions.

TRADE STATISTICS FOR SELECTED COUNTRIES

(IN BILLIONS OF U.S. DOLLARS)

Country	Exports	Imports	Trade Balance
Australia	178.9	187.2	
Belgium	372.9	375.2	
Brazil	200.0	176.0	
Canada	461.8	436.7	
China	1,465.0	1,156.0	
Egypt	33.4	56.4	
France	761.0	833.0	
Germany	1,530.0	1,202.0	
India	175.7	287.5	
Israel	54.2	62.5	
Italy	566.1	566.8	
Japan	776.8	696.2	
Malaysia	195.7	156.2	
Mexico	294.0	305.9	
Nigeria	83.1	46.4	
Philippines	49.0	58.0	
Russia	476.0	302.0	
United Kingdom	468.7	645.7	
United States	1,377.0	2,190.0	
Venezuela	103.5	53.4	

Source: The World Factbook, Central Intelligence Agency

Continued on next page

Chapter 4

1. How many countries have a trade deficit (import more than they export)?

_____

_____

2. How many countries have a trade surplus (export more than they import)?

_____

_____

3. Which country had the largest trade surplus?

_____

_____

4. Which country had the largest trade deficit?

_____

_____

5. Which countries had exports and imports each totaling over $1 trillion?

_____

_____

The following questions require answers to be calculated as percentages. To calculate trade balance as a percentage, subtract imports from exports, then divide the answer by exports.

6. What percentage is the United States' trade balance?

_____

_____

7. Expressed as a percentage, which country's trade balance was closest to zero?

_____

_____

8. By percentage, whose trade deficit is larger, India's or the United States'?

_____

_____

9. By percentage, whose trade surplus is larger, Russia's or Germany's?

_____

_____

Name _____ Date _____ Class _____

Chapter 4 Global Opportunities
Academic Integration Activity

Social Studies
Interpreting Bar Graphs

Directions One of the chief aims of the United Nations is to foster cooperation in social and economic development. The UN's Millennium Development Goals seek to eradicate poverty and hunger, raise worldwide educational standards, improve health, fight disease and infant mortality, achieve environmental sustainability, and develop global partnerships for development.

The UN Development Program grants technical and financial assistance worldwide. Africa is a special area of interest for UN projects. The Economic Commission for Africa (UNECA) studies economic trends on the continent and encourages economic cooperation among African member states. The graphs below are from a recent UNECA report and track fiscal deficits among African nations in different categories. Use the information in the two tables to answer the questions that follow.

DISTRIBUTION OF FISCAL DEFICITS IN AFRICA, 2008 (42 total countries)

	Oil-Producing Countries	Non-Oil-Producing Countries	Mineral-Rich	Non-Mineral-Rich	Sub-Saharan Countries
Countries with surpluses	8	4	2	2	10
Less than 5%	2	3	1	2	5
5% to 10%	0	1	1	0	1
More than 10%	6	0	0	0	4
Countries with deficits	5	25	8	17	26
Less than 5%	4	18	5	13	5
5% to 10%	1	5	2	3	19
More than 10%	0	2	1	1	2
Total Number of Countries	13	29	10	19	36

Continued on next page

Chapter 4

DISTRIBUTION OF FISCAL DEFICITS IN AFRICA
BY RESOURCE GROUP, 1998-2007 (42 total countries)

	Oil-Producing Countries	Non-Oil-Producing Countries	Mineral-Rich	Non-Mineral-Rich
Countries with surpluses	7	2	1	1
Less than 5%	1	1	0	1
5% to 10%	3	1	1	0
More than 10%	3	0	0	0
Countries with deficits	6	27	9	18
Less than 5%	5	23	7	16
5% to 10%	1	3	2	1
More than 10%	0	1	0	1
Total Number of Countries	13	29	10	19

Source: United Nations Economic Commission for Africa

1. How many countries in the study are not Sub-Saharan?

    A 0
    B 3
    C 5
    D 6

2. How many countries produce oil?

    A 7
    B 8
    C 13
    D 29

3. From comparing the tables, which statement is true?

    A More oil and non-oil producing countries had surpluses in 2008 than in the previous decade.
    B Fewer oil and non-oil producing countries had surpluses in 2008 than in the previous decade.

4. How many non-mineral-rich countries had a budget deficit of less than 5% in 2008?

    A 9
    B 13
    C 17v
    D 18

5. From comparing the tables, which statement is true?

    A The general trend in Africa is toward higher deficits.
    B The general trend in Africa is toward lower deficits.

Chapter 4 Global Opportunities

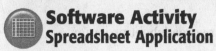

Software Activity
Spreadsheet Application

Directions The objective of this activity is to calculate population growth in selected foreign markets.

Imagine you are the owner of a manufacturing plant that produces personal digital assistants (PDAs). You feel that the domestic market has become almost saturated and offers little opportunity for large increases in sales. As a result, you are examining foreign markets for export opportunities. You would like to begin exporting PDAs to at least one foreign country by the beginning of next year. You need to act fast!

Based on market and economic factors, you have narrowed your choices to the countries listed below. One factor that will have a dramatic impact on your decision will be the growth rate in population. You have collected data on current population totals, as well as population counts from five years ago.

The printout below shows data that you have collected. Calculate the growth rate for each country by dividing the difference in population totals by the population from five years ago.

Country	Population (5 years ago)	Current Population	Growth Rate
Argentina	38,640,207	40,482,395	
Belarus	9,854,231	9,689,800	
Dominica	71,727	72,660	
Estonia	1,372,023	1,340,415	
Ghana	22,414,198	23,832,495	
Jamaica	2,712,489	2,825,928	
Martinique	393,210	402,852	
Qatar	802,304	1,652,608	
South Africa	46,935,819	47,901,232	

Continued on next page

Spreadsheet Directions

1. Start your spreadsheet software program.

2. Re-create the table from the previous page using your spreadsheet program.

3. Enter a formula to calculate growth rate for each of the countries listed.

4. After completing your calculations, save your work.

5. Print out a copy of your work if your teacher has instructed you to do so.

6. Answer the following questions.

Interpreting Results

1. Which country has the largest growth rate?

_____

_____

2. Which country has the smallest growth rate?

_____

_____

_____

Drawing Conclusions

3. Should you begin your export program to the country with the largest growth rate? Why or why not?

_____

_____

_____

_____

4. Based on the data presented, which of these countries would be least desirable for your export program? Explain.

_____

_____

_____

_____

Chapter 4 Global Opportunities

 Test Prep
Understanding Essay Test Words

Directions Read the tips for understanding essay test words, then answer the questions.

UNDERSTANDING ESSAY TEST WORDS
Verbs are key words in essay test questions and directions. Note the differences between the meanings of these verbs, and keep them in mind when completing an essay test or assignment: • To *evaluate* means to look at the limitations and contributions of an idea. • To *explain* means to make the meaning of an idea clear. • To *justify* means to give reasons why an idea was stated. • To *outline* means to list the main points of an idea. • To *summarize* means to give a shortened version of an idea.

1. Summarize the reasons for the growth of the global economy.

_____

_____

_____

_____

_____

2. Explain why it is easier for foreign companies to trade in China than in Japan.

_____

_____

_____

_____

_____

3. Outline the questions entrepreneurs should ask themselves before entering international trade.

_____

_____

_____

_____

_____

Chapter 4

Chapter 5 Feasibility and Business Planning

 Note Taking

Directions As you read, write notes, facts, and main ideas in the note-taking column. Write key words and short phrases in the cues column. Then summarize the section in the summary box.

Cues	Note Taking
• business concept	**FEASIBILITY ANALYSIS: TESTING AN OPPORTUNITY** • A business concept focuses your thinking on four elements: 1. the product or service; 2. the customer; 3. the benefit; 4. distribution of benefit.
• business plan	**THE BUSINESS PLAN** • A business plan gives a complete, detailed picture of a new business and the strategy to launch the business.
Summary	

Chapter 5 Feasibility and Business Planning

Section 5.1 Feasibility Analysis: Testing an Opportunity

Section Review: Apply

Directions How you present yourself and your business is important to potential investors, bankers, and customers. The name that you select should help sell your product. A good business name should be memorable, and it should communicate what the business is all about. If the quality of your business is revealed in the name, you will be advertising your product every time people see the name of your business.

This activity presents business descriptions and corresponding business names. Evaluate each example and determine if the name is memorable and communicates the nature of the business. If not, create a new name for the company. If the name is a good one for the business being described explain why you think the name does not need to be changed. An example is given to help you get started.

Business Description	Business Name	Revised Name/Explanation
Example: *Bookstore with an attached café*	*Nickleby's Bookstore and Café*	Name is memorable (invokes a Dickens novel) and communicates the type of business.
1. Coffee house specializing in cheesecakes	The Coffee Table	
2. Frame shop	The Frame Station	
3. Bookstore that specializes in rare books	The Book Escape	
4. Interior decorator specializing in window treatments	Inside Looking Out	

Chapter 5

5. Lawn care service	The Lawn Doctor	
6. An upscale used-furniture store (sells reproductions and near-antiques at reasonable prices)	Delectable Collectibles	
7. Movie theater and café	Cinema Sensations	
8. Service that comes to a customer's home to do auto oil changes	Presto Oil Change	
9. Catering service that delivers low-calorie lunches to businesses	Diets to Go	
10. Service that prepares and serves candlelight dinners in customers' homes	Richard's Upscale Catering	
11. Service that cares for pets in the owner's home while the owner is away	Pam's Pet Care	

Chapter 5

Chapter 5 Feasibility and Business Planning
Section 5.2 The Business Plan
Section Review: Analyze

Directions You can format a business plan in many ways as long as you include the sections that investors, bankers, and others expect to see. This activity will present you with the opportunity to define and create an outline of the sections that you will need in a business plan.

1. Write short descriptions for each of the sections of a business plan that are listed below. The Executive Summary section is completed for you.

Executive Summary

_____

_____

_____

Management Team Plan

_____

_____

_____

Company Description

_____

_____

_____

Product and Service Plan

_____

_____

_____

Vision and Mission Statements

_____

_____

_____

Continued on next page

Industry Overview

_____

_____

Market Analysis

_____

_____

Competitive Analysis

_____

_____

_____

Marketing Plan

_____

_____

_____

Operational Plan

_____

_____

_____

Organizational Plan

_____

_____

_____

Financial Plan

_____

_____

_____

Growth Plan

_____
_____
_____

Contingency Plan

_____
_____
_____
_____

Cover Page

_____
_____
_____
_____

Title Page

_____
_____
_____
_____

Table of Contents

_____
_____
_____
_____

Supporting Documents

_____
_____
_____
_____

2. Use the sections to write an outline of a business plan. The Executive Summary section is completed for you as an example.

_____
_____

I. Executive Summary
_____

A. Name of business
_____

1. Brief statement that describes business
_____

Continued on next page

Chapter 5

   B. Key points

      1. Key point #1

      2. Key point #2

      3. Key point #3

   C. Sharp and concise wrap-up

3. What might determine how you arrange the sections of a business plan? Explain your answer by giving an example.

_____

_____

_____

_____

_____

4. Describe the three steps in developing a business plan.
   Step 1: Make a Research Plan and Gather Data

_____

_____

_____

_____

_____

   Step 2: Set Up a Notebook to Organize Your Data

_____

_____

_____

_____

_____

   Step 3: Write a Draft

_____

_____

_____

_____

Chapter 5

Chapter 5 Feasibility and Business Planning

Software Activity
Database Application

Directions The objective of this activity is to evaluate customer responses to a questionnaire.

The Acme Model Company recently completed a marketing research survey. The purpose of the survey was to learn about customers' opinions and attitudes toward the firm. The customers' responses were all recorded in a database. The question to which customers responded are as follows.

How would you rate the service in this store?
    a. Excellent
    b. Above Average
    c. Average
    d. Below Average
    e. Poor

Please indicate your age category:
    a. 21 and under
    b. 22–35
    c. 36–45
    d. 46–55
    e. over 55

On the printout below, you will find the responses to these questions.

Customer	Age Category	M/F	Question Response
1	A	M	A
2	B	F	A
3	A	M	B
4	A	M	A
5	E	F	A
6	D	F	D
7	E	F	E
8	A	M	B
9	B	M	A
10	A	M	A
11	E	F	E
12	D	F	B
13	A	M	A
14	B	M	A
15	C	M	A

Continued on next page

Chapter 5

Database Directions

1. Start your database software program.

2. Re-create the table from the previous page using your spreadsheet program.

3. Sort the responses for question #1 by type of response. The database will sort these responses alphabetically.

4. Save your sorted database.

5. Print out a copy of your work if your teacher has instructed you to do so.

6. Answer the following questions.

Interpreting Results

1. How many customers responded with "excellent" to question #1? Did these customers fall into any type of age or gender pattern?

_____

_____

2. How many customers responded with "below average" or "poor"? Did these customers fall into any type of age or gender pattern?

_____

_____

Drawing Conclusions

3. If these 15 customers represent the typical customers at Acme Model Company, what are some general characteristics of these customers?

_____

_____

4. Based on these responses, what recommendations would you make to the owner of Acme Model Company?

_____

_____

_____

_____

_____

_____

_____

Chapter 5

Chapter 5 Feasibility and Business Planning

Academic Integration Activity

English Language Arts
Reading Skills

Directions Match each content vocabulary term to its definition by writing the corresponding letter on the line provided.

a. beneficiaries	**h.** distribution channel	**o.** prototype
b. benefit	**i.** executive summary	**p.** Small Business Administration (SBA)
c. business concept	**j.** feasibility analysis	**q.** target customer
d. business model	**k.** feature	**r.** trade association
e. business plan	**l.** indirect channel	**s.** value chain
f. competitive matrix	**m.** industry	**t.** vision statement
g. direct channel	**n.** mission statement	

_____ **1.** Something that promotes or enhances the value of a product or service to the customer

_____ **2.** A brief recounting of the key points contained in a business plan

_____ **3.** An analysis that helps an entrepreneur decide whether a new business concept has potential

_____ **4.** Working model of a new product

_____ **5.** This describes how you intend to create and capture value with your business concept.

_____ **6.** Section of a business plan that establishes the scope and purpose of a company

_____ **7.** Part of developing a business concept, this is a tool that organizes important information about potential competition.

_____ **8.** Means by which a business delivers a product or service to customers

Chapter 5

_____ **9.** Distinctive aspect, quality, or characteristic of a product or service

_____ **10.** Federal agency that provides service to small businesses and new entrepreneurs

_____ **11.** A clear and concise description of a business opportunity

_____ **12.** Distribution channel through which a product or service flows from the producer to the customer

_____ **13.** Offers assistance to entrepreneurs in a specific profession or industry

_____ **14.** Group of businesses with a common interest

_____ **15.** In a market, the end-users of a product or service

_____ **16.** Document that presents a complete and detailed picture of a new business, as well as a strategy to start the business

_____ **17.** In an operational plan, a way of delivering a product or service directly to a customer

_____ **18.** Expresses the specific aspirations and major goal of a company

_____ **19.** Distribution method in which a product or service is delivered to the customer through a wholesaler

_____ **20.** Potential customers who are most likely to buy a particular product or service

Chapter 5

Chapter 5 Feasibility and Business Planning

Academic Integration Activity

Social Studies
Classifying Information

Directions Review the nine steps of developing a business concept in the table below. The questions that follow are descriptions of specific steps for two women, Kate and Andrea, who are thinking about starting a gourmet food truck that uses Facebook and Twitter to update customers on its daily location and menu. Write the number of the step that is described in the blank that follows. The first is done for you.

Step 1	Write a Concept Statement
Step 2	Test the Concept in the Market
Step 3	Test the Industry
Step 4	Talk to Customers—the Market
Step 5	Test Product or Service Requirements
Step 6	Evaluate the Founding Team
Step 7	Study the Competition
Step 8	Look at Start-Up Resource Needs
Step 9	Analyze the Value Chain

1. Kate is an experienced chef who has run a restaurant kitchen. Andrea has cooking experience and used to own a coffee shop. _____Step 6_____

2. The city Kate and Andrea live in is very tech savvy. Many potential customers have told them a "wired" food truck is a great idea. _____

3. Andrea considered the benefits and features of the business concept, then typed out a description of the business concept. _____

4. They studied the trends and overall health of the food truck business. _____

5. They researched the price of a truck and the cost of outfitting it with a kitchen. _____

6. They performed a feasibility analysis to determine if their concept had potential. _____

7. Kate created a matrix that listed their potential competitors' customers, benefits, strengths, and weaknesses. _____

8. They researched the most cost-effective ways of acquiring quality meats, produce, and condiments. _____

9. Kate drew a blueprint of their ideal food truck to see how much room would be needed to quickly and effectively make gourmet dishes. _____

Chapter 5

Chapter 5 Feasibility and Business Planning
Case Study Activity

Solid Waste Recovery

Directions Read the *BusinessWeek* Case Study feature in this chapter of your textbook. Then study the tables below and complete the Case Study Activity. Complete Table 2 (the first row is completed for you) and answer the questions that follow.

TABLE 1: UNITED STATES SOLID WASTE GENERATION STATISTICS

Year	Total Solid Waste Generation Before Recycling (million tons)	Per Capita Generation (pounds per person per day)
1960	88.1	2.68
1970	121.1	3.25
1980	151.6	3.66
1990	205.2	4.50
2000	239.1	4.65
2007 (most recent data available)	254.1	4.62

Source: Environmental Protection Agency

TABLE 2: GENERATION AND RECOVERY (RECYCLED OR COMPOSTED) OF MUNICIPAL SOLID WASTE MATERIALS, 2007
(in millions of tons)
(Partial List)

Material	Weight Generated	Weight Recovered	Recovery Percentage
Paper and Paperboard	83.0	45.20	54.5%
Glass	13.6	3.22	
Metals	20.8	7.23	
Plastics	30.7	2.09	
Rubber and Leather	7.48	1.10	
Textiles	11.9	1.90	
Wood	14.2	1.32	
Other Materials and Wastes	72.43	28.86	
Total	254.1	90.9	

1. In Table 1, what trend is shown in the data regarding per capita solid waste generation?

   Pounds increased every year.

2. In Table 2, which material has the lowest recovery percentage?

   Rubber & Leather

3. What percentage of total weight generated is plastic? What percentage of total weight recovered is plastic?

   30.7 is generated plastic, 2.09 is the weight recovered

4. The data in these tables were collected before Metabolix's bioplastic product Mirel became commercially available. Why is Mirel important for solid waste recovery efforts?

   _____

   _____

   _____

   _____

   _____

   _____

   _____

5. If Mirel becomes the plastic of choice for businesses and consumers, what changes would you expect in solid waste generation and recovery statistics in 10 years?

   _____

   _____

   _____

   _____

   _____

   _____

   _____

   _____

Chapter 5 Feasibility and Business Planning

Test Prep
Using Flash Cards

Directions Use the chart below to help you create question-and-answer flash cards to use as study aids before taking tests. Then transfer the information onto flash cards. Use the following information to create the cards:

- Use 3" by 5" index cards.
- Create questions from headings, key words, end-of-section questions, end-of-chapter questions, and any questions in the text or margins. Write your question on one side of the index card.
- On the back of the index card, write the answer to the question.
- Review the cards in random order. Look at the front of the card. Read the question aloud, then answer the question.
- Turn the card over to review the answer.

FRONT OF CARD (QUESTION)	BACK OF CARD (ANSWER)
What is a business concept?	A clear and concise description of an opportunity, including the product or service, the customer, the benefit, and the distribution.

Chapter 6 Market Analysis

 Note Taking

Directions As you read, write notes, facts, and main ideas in the note-taking column. Write key words and short phrases in the cues column. Then summarize the section in the summary box.

Cues	Note Taking
	DOING MARKET RESEARCH
• industry	• Industry: collection of businesses categorized by specific business activity
• trends	**INDUSTRY AND MARKET ANALYSIS**
	• Industry forces affect ability to do business.

Summary

Chapter 6 Market Analysis
Section 6.1 Doing Market Research
Section Review: Identify

Directions The first step in doing a market analysis is identification of your market. Your market is the group of people or companies who have a demand for your product and are willing and able to buy it. In order to make the most effective and efficient appeal to potential customers, you should divide the total market into smaller segments. You can then appeal to the special interests or needs of one of those segments—your target market.

Market analysts have coined terms to refer to specific market segments. Some of these are listed below and on the next page. For each group listed, identify three specialized goods or services that would have a special appeal, then explain why.

Target Group	Description
1. Dinks	Double income, no kids

a. _____

b. _____

c. _____

Explain:

_____

_____

_____

_____

2. Woofs	Well-off, over fifty

a. _____

b. _____

c. _____

Explain:

_____

_____

_____

_____

Target Group	Description
3. Skippies	School kids with income and purchasing power

   a. _____

   b. _____

   c. _____

Explain:

_____

_____

_____

_____

_____

4. Swaks	Single woman and kids

   a. _____

   b. _____

   c. _____

Explain:

_____

_____

_____

_____

_____

_____

5. Swank	Single woman and no kids

   a. _____

   b. _____

   c. _____

Explain:

_____

_____

_____

_____

_____

_____

_____

Chapter 6 Market Analysis
Section 6.2 Industry and Market Analysis
Section Review: Research

Directions In Chapter 6, you read about market research, the process for investigating an idea for a product or business. This activity will give you an opportunity to apply the market research process you learned.

The idea is to start a store called Your Very Own Sofa, where customers come to design a sofa their way. In other words, customers will have the option to choose "this arm," "that leg," "this cushion," or "that fabric." Get the idea? Customers will custom-design their sofas to suit their own tastes, color schemes, and lifestyles.

Based on the steps for market research, you are to define the problem and describe how you might go about conducting market research for this business idea. Follow the guidelines and questions below to organize your thinking. If you do not have enough room for your answers, use additional sheets of paper.

1. **Define the problem.** What do you need to examine? What are the specific questions that you want to answer?

   _____

   _____

   _____

2. **Select a research approach.** Give a reason for the approach that you choose and the type of information you will collect.

   _____

   _____

   _____

3. **Gather information.** How will you gather information? If you are using secondary research, what sources are available to you? If you are conducting a survey, how will you determine who will be asked to participate? What are the other considerations when you begin to gather information?

   _____

   _____

   _____

   _____

4. **Conduct primary research.** Imagine that you decide to conduct a survey to determine if people would purchase a sofa from this type of business. On a separate sheet of paper, identify five questions that you think are critical in determining the viability of this business. Explain why each question is important. What will the answers tell you about your business? An example is provided to help you get started.

Survey question: *When is the last time you purchased a new sofa?*

Rationale: *The interviewer may learn how often people purchase sofas, if they are in need of a new sofa, and how many people purchase sofas.*

Survey Question 1: _____

_____

Rationale: _____

_____

_____

Survey Question 2: _____

_____

Rationale: _____

_____

_____

Survey Question 3: _____

_____

Rationale: _____

_____

_____

Survey Question 4: _____

_____

Rationale: _____

_____

_____

Survey Question 5: _____

_____

Rationale: _____

_____

_____

Chapter 6 Market Analysis

Software Activity
Database Application

Directions The objective of this activity is to develop a customer profile for a business.

Businesses can no longer be successful with the strategy of trying to be all things to all people—they must focus. Entrepreneurs must clearly define the type of customer they are trying to reach. Business owners should also routinely monitor their customers to determine if they are reaching their target market.

Imagine you are a storeowner who wishes to develop a profile of frequent shoppers. You have just started collecting data from your customers. During the first hour of surveying, 20 customers were interviewed, and their responses are recorded on the printout below. The following demographic data is reported:

- gender (M or F)
- age (A=Under 21, B=21–35, C=36–45, D=46–55, E=Over 55)
- zip code
- income range (A=Under $25,000, B=$25,000–$45,000, C=Over $45,000)
- family size

Customer	Gender of Respondent	Age Group of Respondent	Zip Code	Income Range	Family Size
1	M	A	29204	A	1
2	M	A	29211	A	1
3	M	B	29204	A	2
4	M	B	29211	B	2
5	F	C	29208	B	3
6	F	E	29208	C	2
7	M	D	29204	C	4
8	F	D	29204	B	3
9	M	B	29211	B	1
10	M	B	29208	B	1
11	M	B	29204	B	1
12	F	C	29204	B	2
13	F	D	29211	C	2
14	F	E	29204	B	5
15	F	D	29204	C	3
16	M	A	29210	B	1
17	M	A	29208	A	1
18	M	E	29211	B	2
19	M	C	29211	C	2
20	M	B	29204	A	1

Database Directions

1. Start your database software program.

2. Re-create the table from the previous page using your spreadsheet program.

3. Sort the data by each of the following categories—sex, age, zip code, income, and family size. After each sort, save your work.

4. Print out a copy of your work if your teacher has instructed you to do so.

5. Answer the following questions.

Interpreting Results

1. Based on the data presented, describe the profile of your core customer.

   _____

   _____

   _____

2. Why is it important to know your customers' zip codes? How can entrepreneurs use their data?

   _____

   _____

   _____

   _____

3. Why is it so important for an entrepreneur to develop a customer profile?

   _____

   _____

   _____

Drawing Conclusions

4. How does it benefit entrepreneurs to monitor their customers periodically to determine whether or not they match their target market?

   _____

   _____

   _____

   _____

Chapter 6

Chapter 6 Market Analysis

Academic Integration Activity

 English Language Arts
Synonyms and Antonyms

Directions Look at the word pairs below. One of the words is from Chapter 6. Mark each pair **S** if the words are similar in meaning (synonyms) or **A** if they are closer to being opposite (antonyms). On the line following each pair, tell why you marked the words as you did.

1. _____ prospective/considered

_____

2. _____ perspective/understanding

_____

3. _____ chaotic/peaceful

_____

4. _____ instablility/order

_____

5. _____ cater/serve

_____

6. _____ variable/constant

_____

7. _____ unbiased/prejudiced

_____

8. _____ conundrum/problem

_____

9. _____ fragmented/together

_____

10. _____ intermediaries/agents

_____

11. _____ emancipated/captured

_____

12. _____ foothold/support

_____

Name <u>Julian Ford</u> Date _____ Class _____

Chapter 6 Market Analysis
Academic Integration Activity

Social Studies
Value Chains

Directions The U.S. automobile industry is a classic example of a well-defined value chain. The auto manufacturer is the most visible business in the production of a car, but it is really just one business in an extensive value chain—all the businesses that deal with other businesses in an industry.

Read the descriptions of the different parts of the value chain. Fill in the flow chart with the parts of the value chain in the correct order. One oval is filled in for you. Then answer the question on the following page.

- **Distribution and Sales:** After production is complete, automobiles are shipped to dealerships around the world to be sold.
- **Parts:** Tires, windshields, and air bags are examples of parts.
- **Raw Materials:** These include rubber, glass, steel, plastic, and aluminum.
- **Assembly:** Automakers are looking for ways to cut costs out of the manufacturing process. Recent trends to reduce costs include using fewer parts in each vehicle component, minimizing industrial waste and pollution, and having parts delivered to assembly plants on a just-in-time basis.
- **Design:** Automakers use consumer research to begin designing models to meet public demand.
- **Marketing:** Automakers and individual dealers work together to create national, regional, and local marketing strategies. These may include television and radio advertising or special incentives offered to customers. In addition, firms have started to advertise more online.

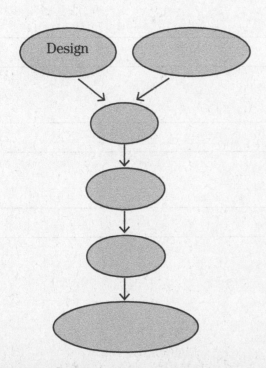

Continued on next page

1. Use library and Internet research to identify companies that might be part of the U.S. automobile industry value chain. Try to find at least two examples for each category.

   a. Distribution: automobile shippers

   _____

   _____

   b. Sales: dealerships

   _____

   _____

   c. Assembly: environmental consultants

   _____

   _____

   d. Raw Materials: steel

   _____

   _____

   e. Raw Materials: aluminum

   _____

   _____

   f. Marketing: advertising agencies

   _____

   _____

   g. Design: consumer research firms

   _____

   _____

   h. Parts: tires

   _____

   _____

Chapter 6 Market Analysis
Case Study Activity
Twittering for Business

Directions Read the *BusinessWeek* Case Study feature in this chapter of your textbook. Then read the article below and answer the questions that follow.

HOW TO SPEAK TWITTER: A TWITTER GLOSSARY
By Ian Paul

At Reply, or "@reply": A direct tweet sent to another Twitter user.

Hash Tag: The "#" sign. Allows Twitter users to group tweets by topic, making it easier to search particular conversations using Twitter Search.

Link: Including a URL in your tweet.

MisTweet: A tweet one later regrets.

ReTweet: To repost something that's already in the Twitter stream. Usually preceded by "RT" and "@[username]," to give credit to the original poster.

SnapTweet: A tweet that includes a photo taken with a cell phone, uploaded to the photo- sharing Web site Flickr and posted to Twitter via the Web site Snap Tweet.

Twittcrastination: Procrastination brought on by Twitter use.

Twadd: To add someone as a friend or follower.

Twaigslist/Twebay: To sell something on Twitter.

Tweeter/Twitterer: Someone who uses Twitter.

TwinkedIn: Inviting friends made on Twitter to connect on the professional networking site LinkedIn.

Twittectomy: To remove someone from the list of people you follow.

Twitterati: The A-list twitterers everyone follows.

Twitterfly: Twitter's version of a social butterfly, marked by the extreme use of @ signs.

Twitterlooing: Twittering from the bathroom.

Twitterpated: Overwhelmed with Twitter messages.

(From BusinessWeek, April 3, 2009)

Continued on next page

1. Do you or anyone you know use Twitter? If yes, how do you and/or they use Twitter?

   _____

   _____

   _____

   _____

2. Imagine you are on a social networking site and receive a "tweet" or similar kind of message advertising a sale on a product or service. Would you be more or less likely to look into the deal than you would if you saw a similar ad on television, on the radio, or in print? Explain.

   _____

   _____

   _____

   _____

3. Access Twitter online and go to the page for JetBlue Airways. Use the space below to copy down five recent tweets from the JetBlue page. Then, using the Twitter Glossary and the information you learn from the tweets, write a short explanation of each tweet.

   _____

   _____

   _____

   _____

   _____

4. Observing JetBlue's Twitter page, interpret how the company uses Twitter.

   _____

   _____

   _____

   _____

   _____

Chapter 6 Market Analysis

Test Prep
Multiple-Choice Tests

Directions Read these multiple-choice test strategies. Then use the strategies when you answer the questions shown. Fill in the bubble next to the best answer.

MULTIPLE-CHOICE TEST STRATEGIES

- If you know one of the answer choices is correct, then do not choose "none of the above."
- If you know one of the answer choices is incorrect, then do not choose "all of the above."
- A positive answer choice is more likely to be correct than a negative answer choice.

---

1. A feature that makes a product more desirable than its competitors' products is a _____.

   - ◯ market share
   - ◯ brand loyalty
   - ◯ competitive advantage
   - ◯ none of the above

2. Ways to segment a market include _____.

   - ◯ demographics
   - ◯ psychographics
   - ◯ buying characteristics
   - ◯ all of the above

3. An industry's life cycle includes _____.

   - ◯ birth
   - ◯ growth
   - ◯ maturity
   - ◯ decline
   - ◯ all of the above

4. Market research does not involve _____.

   - ◯ defining a research question
   - ◯ developing a business concept
   - ◯ looking at secondary resources
   - ◯ talking directly to the customer

5. All of the following are types of market research except _____.

- ○ process
- ○ historic
- ○ exploratory
- ○ description

6. The correct order for market research is _____.

- ○ information needs, secondary research, primary research, organize, and analyze
- ○ secondary research, primary research, information needs, organize, and analyze
- ○ organize, analyze, primary research, secondary research, information needs
- ○ information needs, primary research, secondary research, organize, and analyze

7. You can learn about your company's competitive advantage by _____.

- ○ visiting competitors' outlets
- ○ buying competitors' products
- ○ searching the Internet and your competitors' Web sites
- ○ all of the above

8. All of the following are barriers to entry except _____.

- ○ economies of scale
- ○ market strategy
- ○ brand loyalty
- ○ government regulation

9. To research your competition, you should look at _____.

- ○ competitive advantage
- ○ strengths and weaknesses
- ○ marketing strategy
- ○ all of the above

10. To build a customer profile you need to know _____.

- ○ who is the customer
- ○ how often they buy
- ○ how your business can meet their needs
- ○ all of the above

Chapter 7 Types of Business Ownership

 Note Taking

Directions As you read, write notes, facts, and main ideas in the note-taking column. Write key words and short phrases in the cues column. Then summarize the section in the summary box.

Cues	Note Taking
• sole proprietorship: business owned and operated by one person	**SOLE PROPRIETORSHIPS AND PARTNERSHIPS** • 76 percent of U.S. businesses are sole proprietorships.
• corporation: business registered by a state and which operates apart from its owners	**CORPORATIONS** • Continue after owners have sold interests or passed away.
Summary	

Chapter 7 Types of Business Ownership

Section 7.1 Sole Proprietorships and Partnerships

Section Review: Apply

Directions Read the scenario and answer the questions that follow.

Situation Amar and Adina had known each other for a long time. Adina wanted to open a store featuring original wood carvings. She also wanted to sell tools and other carving products. She knew that Amar was a good wood carver, but he had little interest in running a business. However, Amar had the resources needed to begin such a business. With Adina's business sense, knowledge of the field, and enthusiasm, she knew she could make it work. All she needed was Amar's interest in wood carving, his contacts with other carvers, and his financial resources.

When Adina approached Amar with the idea, he was interested but a little skeptical. She had suggested that he become a limited partner so he would not have to be involved with running the business. Amar wanted more. He wanted a full partnership, with its shared responsibility for decision making. They seemed to be at odds until Adina presented a solution.

1. Why do you think Amar was not happy when Adina suggested that he become a limited partner?

   _____

   _____

   _____

   _____

   _____

2. What do you think Adina's solution was? Hint: Refer to Chapter 7, and review the elements that lead to the greatest potential for partnership access.

   _____

   _____

   _____

   _____

   _____

   _____

You are now Amar and Adina's attorney. They have asked you to draw up a partnership agreement for them. Using the headings that appear on the following two pages as a guide, develop a partnership agreement that you believe Adina and Amar would sign. You will need to use your imagination in developing this contract.

Name of Business: _____

Purpose: _____

_____

_____

_____

_____

Duration of Agreement: _____

_____

_____

Character of Partners (general or limited, active or silent): _____

_____

_____

_____

Business Expenses (how handled): _____

_____

_____

_____

_____

Division of Profits and Losses: _____

_____

_____

_____

_____

Continued on next page

Chapter 7

Salaries: _____
_____
_____
_____
_____

Death of a Partner: _____
_____
_____
_____
_____
_____

Handling of Business Disagreements: _____
_____
_____
_____
_____
_____

Responsibilities of a Partner: _____
_____
_____
_____
_____
_____

Other Additions (anything else that you think should be included): _____
_____
_____
_____
_____
_____
_____

Chapter 7 Types of Business Ownership

Section 7.2 Corporations

Section Review: Plan

Directions Select a type of business that you might want to start. Then follow the steps below to complete this activity, using the chart provided. A generic sample is given to help you get started.

- Think of the businesses in your area that are the type you may want to start. List four of them.
- Identify the type of ownership for each business that you list. (This may require some research.)
- For each business, list an advantage and disadvantage for the particular form of ownership.

Type of business: _____

Name of Business	Form of Ownership	Advantage of Form of Ownership for This Business	Disadvantage of Form of Ownership for This Business
Example: *Max & Mabel's*	*Corporation*	*Easier to Raise Money*	*Fees and restrictions*
1.			
2.			
3.			
4.			

Chapter 7 Types of Business Ownership

Software Activity
PowerPoint Application

Directions The objective of this activity is to contrast the advantages and disadvantages of the different types of business ownership.

Before starting a business, potential entrepreneurs must determine the most appropriate form of organization for their new firm. They should carefully analyze the advantages and disadvantages of each type of organization before making a decision. No one type of organization will be best for all types of businesses.

Identify advantages and disadvantages of the following types of business organizations—sole proprietorship, partnership, and corporation. Write your lists as clearly and concisely as possible. You do not have to use complete sentences; however, the statements need to be easily interpreted by others.

You will use this information in developing a slide presentation that will compare the advantages and disadvantages of each type of business organization. First, develop a title slide. Then, for each type of business organization, develop a two-column slide with one column of text describing the advantages, and another column describing the disadvantages.

Advantages	Disadvantages
_____	_____
_____	_____
_____	_____
_____	_____
_____	_____
_____	_____
_____	_____
_____	_____
_____	_____
_____	_____
_____	_____
_____	_____

PowerPoint Directions

1. Start your PowerPoint software program.

2. Based on the information you have collected about the advantages and disadvantages of the types of business organization, develop three slides to include a slide for each type of business organization. The slides should be created with two columns of text, listing the advantages on one column and the disadvantages on the other.

3. Save your work.

4. Print out a copy of your slides if your teacher has instructed you to do so.

5. Answer the following questions.

Interpreting Results

1. For which type of business organization did you list the most advantages? The most disadvantages?

_____

_____

2. Exchange a copy of your slide presentation with a classmate. Check to determine if the advantages and disadvantages were concisely and clearly written. Describe the similarities between the two slide presentations. Describe the differences between the two slide presentations.

_____

_____

_____

Drawing Conclusions

3. Based on your slide presentation, should entrepreneurs select the type of organization that has the most advantages listed? Explain.

_____

_____

4. Based on the information presented in your slide presentation, which type of business organization would be best for someone who wants to open an ice skating rink?

_____

_____

_____

Chapter 7

Chapter 7 Types of Business Ownership
Academic Integration Activity

 **Mathematics**
Calculating Start-Up Expenses

Directions In recent years, music listeners have increasingly turned to buying their favorite songs online. The effect of this trend has been to put many traditional or "brick and mortar" music retailers out of business. Darcy Agosto thinks she has identified a niche market—sophisticated music lovers who are willing to pay more for the superior audio quality and artwork found on old-style vinyl records—that will allow her to start a record store that can succeed in this new business environment.

As a sole proprietor who plans to hire no employees, Darcy is responsible for keeping track of sales and returns, ordering and monitoring inventory, setting prices, and estimating and paying for expenses such as utilities, supplies, and insurance. Review and complete the following table. Then answer the questions that follow. Show your work.

Needle in the Groove Records	
Start-Up Expenses	**Estimated Cost**
rent	$ 1,850
equipment	3,500
office supplies	750
furniture and record racks	5,000
inventory (records and turntable equipment)	35,500
insurance	4,200
security system	595
Total	_____

1. If Darcy cuts her highest expense by one-fifth, how much would the total expenses be afterward?

_____

_____

2. Suppose Darcy must pick a different location for the business. The rent there is 12.75% higher. How much would the total start-up expenses be?

_____

3. To attract customers to the store, Darcy decides to spend three-quarters less on equipment to cover the costs of advertising. How much will be spent for advertising? How much will be spent on equipment?

_____

_____

Chapter 7 Types of Business Ownership
Academic Integration Activity

Science
Burning Calories

Directions Studies show that standards of living and life expectancy are directly related. Jeffrey Fuentes and Carli Smith have taken what they learned as personal trainers for a corporate chain of gyms and formed a business partnership. Their company provides personal fitness coaching. When counseling clients, Jeffrey and Carli use data like the type shown in the table below. Study the table and use it to answer the questions.

CALORIES BURNED PER MINUTE OF ACTIVITY

Activity	120 lbs.	140 lbs.	160 lbs.	180 lbs.
Aerobics	7.4	8.6	9.8	11.1
Basketball	7.5	8.8	10.0	11.3
Cycling (10 mph)	5.5	6.4	7.3	8.2
Hiking	4.5	5.2	6.0	6.7
Jogging	9.3	10.8	12.4	13.9
Running	11.4	13.2	15.1	17.0
Sitting Quietly	1.2	1.3	1.5	1.7
Swimming	7.8	9.0	10.3	11.6
Walking	6.5	7.6	8.7	9.7
Weight Training	6.6	7.6	8.7	9.8

1. If you weigh about 160 lbs. and like to play basketball, how many calories will you burn by playing for 20 minutes? _____ For 35 minutes? _____

2. You and a friend equally divide and eat 10 miniature peanut butter cups. Each cup has 36 calories. You both weigh approximately 120 lbs. If you both jogged for 20 minutes, would that be enough to burn the calories you consumed?

_____

3. How many calories would a 140-lb. person burn with an exercise session consisting of 10 minutes of jogging, 10 minutes of swimming, and 15 minutes of weight training?

_____

4. To lose one pound, you must burn 3,500 excess calories per week, or 500 per day. Assume you are trying to lose 1.5 pounds per week. Find the weight on the table to which yours is closest, pick your favorite exercise activities, and create a daily exercise regimen that will result in a 1.5 pound per week weight loss.

_____

_____

Chapter 7 Types of Business Ownership
Case Study Activity
The Apple iPod

Directions Read the *BusinessWeek* Case Study in this chapter. Then read the information below and complete the Case Study Activity.

It is possible that you can play your digital music and video files on something other than an iPod. But in terms of innovation, units sold (now over 200 million) and cultural impact, Apple Inc.'s product set the standard for digital media players and re-shapes it through continual tinkering.

The iPod was launched on October 23, 2001. The first "Classic" iPod had a maximum capacity of five gigabytes (GB), later increased to 10 GB, and had the patented mechanical wheel that today still allows users to easily access options.

The chart below shows a partial history of iPod models. Use the information from the chart to answer the questions on the next page.

Model	Generation	Maximum Capacity (GB)	Original Release Date (month/year)	Original Retail Cost	Video Enabled?	Wi-fi Available?
Original ("Classic")	first	10	10/01	$499	No	No
	second	20	7/02	$499	No	No
	third	30	4/03	$499	No	No
	fourth	40	7/04	$399	No	No
	fifth	60	10/05	$399	Yes	No
	sixth	160	9/07	$349	Yes	No
Mini	first	4	1/04	$249	No	No
	second	6	2/05	$249	No	No
Nano (replaced Mini)	first	4	9/05	$199	No	No
	second	8	9/06	$199	No	No
	third	8	9/07	$199	Yes	No
	fourth	16	9/08	$299	Yes	No
Shuffle	first	1	1/05	$79	No	No
	second	2	9/06	$79	No	No
	third	4	3/09	$79	No	No
Touch	first	32	9/07	$299	Yes	Yes
	second	32	9/08	$299	Yes	Yes

1. Which iPod model allows users to listen to music, watch video, and access the Internet?

   _____

2. Which is the only iPod model to be discontinued? _____

3. What model replaced it? _____

4. Which iPod model appears to target consumers who want a simple, low-cost device to play music only? _____

5. What general trend do you see in the retail cost of iPods?

   _____

   _____

   _____

   _____

   _____

6. Why do you think the sixth generation iPod Classic (160 GB capacity, video playback capability) has a lower original retail cost than the first generation iPod (10 GB capacity, no video playback)?

   _____

   _____

   _____

   _____

   _____

7. From the information on the table, what dilemma might a potential iPod buyer face when deciding whether to commit to a particular model at a given time? What is an advantage for buyers willing to buy a model or generation with fewer features and less storage capacity?

   _____

   _____

   _____

   _____

   _____

   _____

Chapter 7

Chapter 7 Types of Business Ownership

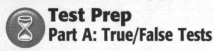

Test Prep
Part A: True/False Tests

Directions Circle *T* for true or *F* for false. Rewrite false statements so that they are true.

1. An. advantage of a sole proprietorship is that it is easy and inexpensive to create. **T   F**

   _____

2. A partnership is the most common business organization involving more than one owner. **T   F**

   _____

3. All partners must sign every contract in a general partnership. **T   F**

   _____

4. The sole proprietorship offers the owner protections from liability. **T   F**

   _____

5. One of the advantages of a sole proprietorship is that it is inexpensive to create. **T   F**

   _____

6. When you use your own name for the business, you need a DBA. **T   F**

   _____

7. A sole proprietorship with more than one owner is termed a partnership. **T   F**

   _____

8. A limited partner has no say over the management of the business. **T   F**

   _____

9. A corporation can live beyond the life of its founders. **T   F**

   _____

10. A nonprofit corporation makes money primarily for the owner's profit. **T   F**

   _____

Part B: Matching

Directions Write the term on the blank line to match each definition with the correct content vocabulary.

sole proprietorship	liability protection	corporation
shareholders	subchapter S corporation	limited liability company (LLC)
unlimited liability	C-corporation	general partner
partnership	nonprofit corporation	limited partner
limited liability		

_____ 1. A business that is owned and operated by one person

_____ 2. Insurance

_____ 3. A partner who risks his or her own investment

_____ 4. The most common corporate form

_____ 5. A legal form that avoids double taxation

_____ 6. Corporate shareholders have this

_____ 7. Corporate owners

_____ 8. Profits remain within the corporation

_____ 9. A hybrid legal form for a business

_____ 10. A business registered by a state and operated apart from its owners

_____ 11. Full responsibility for all debts and actions of a business

_____ 12. An unincorporated business with two or more owners

_____ 13. Responsible for all liability and management

Chapter 7 in right margin

Chapter 8 The Legal Environment

 Note Taking

Directions As you read, write notes, facts, and main ideas in the note-taking column. Write key words and short phrases in the cues column. Then summarize the section in the summary box.

Cues	Note Taking
	LEGAL ISSUES FACING START-UPS
• intellectual property law: laws regulating owner-ship and use of creative works	• Uniform Trade Secrets Act (UTSA) covers trade secrets, the basis of all intellectual property law.
	HANDLING GOVERNMENT REGULATIONS
• Equal Employment Opportunity Commission (EEOC)	• Employers cannot refuse to hire, promote, or give pay increases to an employee based on a number of characteristics.
Summary	

Chapter 8 The Legal Environment
Section 8.1 Legal Issues Facing Start-Ups
Section Review: Apply

Directions Jorge and Eric have decided to start an after-school business. Their school has numerous after-school events in which many parents, teachers, and students are involved. Jorge and Eric noticed that these people often walk to a nearby grocery store to buy snacks and drinks while they are waiting.

The two partners have determined a need and have designed a way to meet it. They want to open a stand that will offer hot food and snacks right on the school grounds. To do so, they will enter into a contract with the school. The contract will include a provision that 20 percent of the stand's profits will be placed in a fund to provide new library books. The remaining profits will be split between the two owner-operators.

Help Jorge and Eric begin their new business by answering the questions below. Imagine that it is you and a friend starting this business. How would you find out what legal requirements you must meet? Hint: Your country or state health departments can answer questions about the legal requirements for food service businesses.

1. What licenses or permits might Jorge and Eric need?

_____

_____

_____

_____

_____

_____

2. What other legal requirements will they need to meet in order to operate their food stand?

_____

_____

_____

_____

_____

_____

_____

Continued on next page

3. In the space below, list the provisions to be included in a contract between Jorge and Eric and the school. Then make a first draft of the contract on a separate sheet of paper.

a. _____

_____

b. _____

_____

c. _____

_____

d. _____

_____

e. _____

_____

f. _____

_____

g. _____

_____

4. In the space below, list the provisions to be included in a contract between Jorge and Eric. Then make a first draft of the contract on a separate sheet of paper. Note: Do not be concerned with their ability to enter into a contract.

a. _____

_____

b. _____

_____

c. _____

_____

d. _____

_____

e. _____

_____

f. _____

_____

g. _____

_____

Chapter 8

Chapter 8 The Legal Environment

Section 8.2 Handling Government Regulations

Section Review: Critical Thinking

Directions Read the information below. Then answer the questions that follow.

Max, owner of Max's Meats, feels that he needs to run a new radio ad to help stimulate sagging sales in his poultry and fish business. This new ad will focus on chicken. He hopes it will bring more people into his store and generate new business. Here is the copy for the new radio ad.

> "Here at Max's Meats, we're having a sale on chickens at our lowest prices ever! These are the plumpest, leanest, healthiest chickens available anywhere. Eating these chickens is guaranteed to lower your cholesterol level and strengthen your heart. Recent reports confirm that eating chicken adds years to your life by reducing the overall fat in your system.

> "At Max's Meats you can now purchase these marvels of culinary delight at unbelievable prices. You will never find a better chicken than this. Hurry over to Max's, the place where stingy shoppers stop in to shop."

Max is not sure where his chickens come from, nor does he know their fat content or their specific health information. While his chicken prices are in fact the lowest in town, his "sale" price is 25 cents higher than his regular price.

Max does know, however, that he will shortly be facing a supply crunch as a result of losses incurred by farmers during a major winter storm. He rationalizes that he can offer turkey or fish at slightly reduced prices if he runs out. He also figures that after running the ad for a few days he can raise his prices to match his competitors' on whatever stock he has left. After all, the ad does not specify for how long the prices are good. Max figures he can just play it by ear.

1. How does this ad and Max's attitude conflict with truth-in-advertising guidelines?

_____

_____

_____

2. If you were to rewrite the ad, what would it say?

_____

_____

_____

_____

_____

_____

Chapter 8 The Legal Environment

Software Activity
Spreadsheet Application

Directions The objective of this activity is to calculate taxes that will be withheld from an employee's pay.

Entrepreneurs must deduct certain payroll taxes from each employee's earnings. Employers are also required to contribute an equal amount to that deducted from each employee's paycheck. This would include the FICA (Federal Insurance Contribution Act), or Social Security tax, as well as federal income taxes. In many state, employers must also deduct state income taxes. All of these taxes are based on a percentage of an employee's gross pay.

Assume that you own a small business. The printout below shows the pay information for employers who work for your firm. The hourly wage and the number of hours worked by each employee are given. Calculate the amount that you should withhold from each employee's paycheck for FICA, federal, and state income taxes. Tax rates are as follows:

FICA Tax Rate—7.65%   State Tax Rate—4.5%   Federal Tax Rate—18.0%

Employee	Hourly Wage	Number of Hours Worked	Gross Pay	FICA Taxes	State Taxes	Federal Taxes	Total Deductions
1	$9.00	40					
2	$8.50	40					
3	$10.25	35					
4	$9.75	37					

Spreadsheet Directions

1. Start your spreadsheet software program.

2. Re-create the table above using your spreadsheet program.

3. Enter the formulas for the first employee to calculate each of the following:
    Gross pay (Hourly wages multiplied by number of hours worked)
    FICA taxes
    State taxes
    Federal taxes
    Total deductions (Add FICA, state, and federal taxes)
    Net Pay (Total deductions subtracted from Gross Pay)
    Copy these formulas to appropriate cells in all remaining rows.

4. After completing your calculations, save your work

5. Print out a copy of your work if your teacher has instructed you to do so.

6. Answer the following questions.

Continued on next page

Chapter 8

Interpreting Results

1. What is the net pay for each of the following employees?
   Net pay is as follows:

   1. _____   3. _____

   2. _____   4. _____

2. Which employee has the highest net pay? The lowest?

   _____

   _____

Drawing Conclusions

3. Why are employers responsible for withholding FICA, state, and federal income taxes from employees' paychecks rather than having each employee pay these taxes at the end of the year?

   _____

   _____

   _____

   _____

   _____

   _____

   _____

   _____

4. Should federal and state governments reimburse business owners for collecting these taxes for them?

   _____

   _____

   _____

   _____

   _____

   _____

   _____

   _____

Name _____ Date _____ Class _____

Chapter 8 The Legal Environment
Academic Integration Activity

 English Language Arts
Reading Skills

Directions Fill in the graphic organizer. The first one is completed for you.

Read the word.	Predict the meaning before reading.	Write a new definition after reading.	Put a check mark [✓] if your definition matches the text's definition.
intellectual property law	Laws regulating property of intellectuals	Group of laws regulating ownership and use of creative works	✓
patent			
patent pending			
copyright			
trademark			
public domain			

permit		
contract		
license		
consideration		
capacity		
wrongful termination		
price discrimination		
bait-and-switch advertising		

Chapter 8

Chapter 8 The Legal Environment

Academic Integration Activity

Social Studies
Laws That Affect Business

Directions Read the passage below about the opening of a business, then answer the questions that follow.

Amy Sweeney had dreamed for years of opening a crafts boutique that would sell products made by local artists. She even had a name—Earth Designs—and knew the shop would concentrate on products made from natural materials. Amy had also spoken to a few artists who agreed to let her sell their work. Finally, she had enough commitments to open her business.

She decided that she would start the business in her garage and would open three days a week—Friday, Saturday, and Sunday. She lived in a nice residential neighborhood, got along well with her neighbors, and saw this as an inexpensive way to begin.

Amy advertised the opening of her shop and was very successful the first weekend. The following week, however, she received a letter informing her that she was violating a number of local laws regarding business operation. In the letter, she was told to shut her boutique immediately.

1. Having read Chapter 8, which local laws do you believe Amy might have violated?

_____

_____

_____

_____

_____

_____

2. Assume Amy did nothing else in starting up her business except what was described above. What legal problems might she encounter?

_____

_____

_____

_____

_____

_____

Chapter 8 The Legal Environment
Case Study Activity
Create an IBM Timeline

Directions Read the *BusinessWeek* Case Study feature in this chapter of the textbook. Then read the passage below and proceed to the next page.

THE EARLY HISTORY OF IBM

International Business Machines Corporation, or IBM, started before the company officially became IBM in 1924. IBM was originally called the Computing Tabulating Recording Corporation (CTR) after a merger of four companies. CTR provided tabulation and employee time-recording systems; manufactured meat slicers and weighing scales; and automatic punch-card systems. The improvement of the punch-card systems would lead to IBM's computer innovations decades later.

A big event in IBM's history was the passage of the Social Security Act in 1935. IBM was hired to maintain employment data for millions of Americans. The company's standard 80-column rectangular-hole punch card, the "IBM Card," introduced in 1928, would be used to run IBM's computers and tabulators for many years to come.

Between 1941 and 1945, when the United States was fighting World War II, IBM expanded its product line to include military rifles, bombsights, and engine parts. All profits from war products were deposited into funds for widows and orphans of IBM employees who died in military service. During the war, IBM built the Harvard Mark I, the U.S.'s first large-scale automatic digital computer.

In the 1950s, IBM developed computers for the U.S. Air Force's automated defense systems, at one point having 7,000 employees working on the project. Innovations during this era included integrated video display, magnetic core memory, multiprocessing, and the first computer networks and algebraic computer language.

In 1964, IBM produced approximately 70% of all computers. Its System/360 mainframes, which at a maximum held 8 megabytes of memory (a tiny fraction of the capacity of today's simplest laptop computers), were purchased by large companies and research facilities.

After refining and building on its existing technology, in 1981 the company introduced the IBM PC, which had a size and price (originally $1,565) that was affordable to individuals and a wide range of businesses. The microcomputer was very popular, but during the 1980s IBM made a business decision widely believed to have cost the company its competitive edge. Instead of developing all of the core components of its machines, such as processors, operating systems, and databases, the company outsourced much of this work to upstarts such as Microsoft and Intel. By the end of the decade, IBM's status as the world's leader in computer innovation was very much in doubt.

Chapter 8

Continued on next page

Directions Use dates and facts from the passage on the previous page to fill in the timeline about IBM.

IBM TIMELINE

1924   1930   1940   1950   1960   1970   1980   1990

Name _____ Date _____ Class _____

Chapter 8 The Legal Environment

Test Prep
Thinking Strategies

Directions Read the thinking strategies, then use the information from the preceding Case Study activity to answer the questions.

THINKING STRATEGIES
• Look at information and problems in new ways and from different perspectives.
• Visualize the information, and create visual representations of the ideas.
• When you do not feel like studying for a test, just do it anyway. Before long you will get into the material.
• Combine thoughts and images, and then rearrange them.

1. What was the original name of IBM?

_____

2. Which early IBM product led to later development of computer systems?

_____

3. Which government legislation was crucial to the growth of IBM?

_____

4. What was the maximum amount of memory that could be held by a System/360 mainframe?

_____

5. Why did the IBM PC appeal to smaller businesses and individuals?

_____

_____

_____

_____

6. How did IBM outsource to other companies? What effect did this have on IBM?

_____

_____

_____

_____

Chapter 9 Site Selection and Layout Planning

 Note Taking

Directions As you read, write notes, facts, and main ideas in the note-taking column. Write key words and short phrases in the cues column. Then summarize the section in the summary

Cues	Note Taking
	COMMUNITY AND SITE SELECTION
• economic base: community's major source of income	• The decision where to place a business determines who sees the business, how they can get to it, and if they will give it a try.
• layout: floor plan or map of business	**LAYOUT PLANNING** • A well-planned layout can enhance a business; a poorly designed layout can hurt it.
Summary	

Chapter 9 Site Selection and Layout Planning

Section 9.1 Community and Site Selection

Section Review: Create

Directions Some businesses are just so offbeat that they invite their creators to defy conventional thinking about many considerations—including site selection. Below is a list of such businesses. Your task is to find an equally offbeat location for each business. (You may even see how some could be incorporated into existing businesses.)

Have fun, and allow your imagination to run wild. However, remember to show a connection between the location and the needs of the business.

1. **Laid-Back Lifestyle Gifts.** This company has a line of products including humorous gear for the "laid-back" golfers, fishers, and hunters. Almost all of the company's merchandise is either funny or fun—and it is all unique.

   _____

   _____

   _____

   _____

2. **Used Tires, USA.** This store sells fashion accessories made from old tires and inner tubes.

   _____

   _____

   _____

   _____

3. **Bento Express.** This Hawaiian-themed restaurant offers teriyaki-laced Spam "sushi" at lunch. It is a big seller.

   _____

   _____

   _____

   _____

Continued on next page

Chapter 9

4. Macaroni Clocks. A brother-and-sister team makes clocks from dried macaroni.

_____

_____

_____

_____

5. Salt Lick City. This store appeals to gourmets who desire more than store-brand salt to sprinkle on their dishes. It sells table salt and sea salt from all over the world—the salt comes in a wide variety of tastes, colors, sizes, and crystal shapes.

_____

_____

_____

_____

_____

6. Designer Bands. This business sells surgical bandages overlaid with different colors of laces, rhinestones, and pearls. The bandages sell for about $2.50 each.

_____

_____

_____

_____

_____

7. The Ravioli Store. This take-out business sells 11 types of freshly-made ravioli at $4.50–$9.99 a pound. Flavors include jalapeño, chocolate, and lobster.

_____

_____

_____

_____

_____

Chapter 9

Chapter 9 Site Selection and Layout Planning
Section 9.2 Layout Planning
Section Review: Plan

Directions The layout of a retail business has a critical impact on sales and, therefore, profits. As you may recall from Chapter 9, the most important design consideration is the flow of customers through the operation.

Below is the layout for an actual public market called The North Market. It currently consists of 28 family-owned businesses. These businesses are engaged primarily in the sale of unprepared foods, such as meat, poultry, produce, and dairy products. The market facility is housed in a World War II surplus Quonset hut. Within this facility, no room exists for expansion of selling space or any addition of businesses.

As you review the layout, pay attention to the number of merchants, aisle exposure, and traffic flow. After you review the market's layout and the types of businesses housed there, answer the questions that follow.

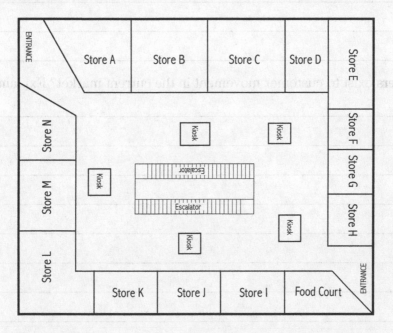

1. How would you describe the layout of merchants within the North Market? Explain.

_____

_____

_____

_____

_____

Continued on next page

Chapter 9

2. Do you think this layout is effective for this type of market facility? Why or why not?

_____

_____

_____

_____

_____

_____

_____

_____

_____

3. Do barriers exist to customer movement in the current market? Explain.

_____

_____

_____

_____

_____

_____

_____

_____

_____

_____

_____

_____

_____

_____

4. Given this type of selling environment, discuss the advantages and disadvantages of product coordination (placing the same type of merchants in the same section of the market).

_____

_____

_____

_____

_____

_____

_____

_____

_____

_____

_____

Chapter 9

Chapter 9 Site Selection and Layout Planning

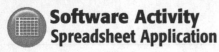

Software Activity
Spreadsheet Application

Directions The objective of this activity is to select a community in which to locate a business.

You are getting ready to open a new store selling "green" clothing and accessories for babies and small children. You have narrowed your selection to three neighborhoods in your city (Belmont, East Point, and Capitol Hill) and have begun to collect demographic data about the locations. In the printout below you will find some of this information.

Before using the data for planning purposes, you will need to calculate the totals of the rows and columns on the printout below.

Demographic Characteristic	Belmont	East Point	Capitol Hill	TOTALS
Sex				
Male	22,567	8,944	11,032	
Female	27,583	10,933	18,941	
Totals				
Age				
Under 14	8,950	6,100	4,950	
15–19	4,900	887	3,100	
20–34	12,250	5,870	6,337	
35–64	17,700	5,990	10,726	
Over 65	6,350	1,030	4,860	
Totals				
Households	18,925	7,587	11,060	
Average Household Size	2.65	2.62	2.71	

Spreadsheet Directions

1. Start your spreadsheet software program.

2. Re-create the table above using your spreadsheet program.

3. Input a formula to calculate the following:
   - total number of males
   - total number of females
   - total number of people in each category
   - total number of households
   - total number of people in each neighborhood

4. Perform the calculations, save your work

5. Print out a copy of your work if your teacher has instructed you to do so.

6. Answer the following questions.

Interpreting Results

1. How many people live in each of the three neighborhoods?

   _____

   _____

2. Based on all the data, which is the largest age category?

   _____

   _____

Drawing Conclusions

3. Some friends have told you that you should locate your store in the neighborhood with the largest population. Do you agree or disagree with this statement? Explain.

   _____

   _____

   _____

   _____

4. Based on the data presented, in which city would you choose to open your "green" children's clothing store?

   _____

   _____

   _____

   _____

Chapter 9

Chapter 9 Site Selection and Layout Planning
Academic Integration Activity

Mathematics
Calculating Square Footage and Acreage

Directions Entrepreneurs must consider lot size when deciding where to put a business. Lots are usually expressed in square feet or, if the lot is large enough, acres.

Imagine that you and a partner have a business selling large amounts of dirt, rocks, mulch, and paving stones to commercial clients such as landscape architects and farmers. Your business has been a success and now it is time to expand to a larger site. You have narrowed your potential sites to three. Calculate square footage, acreage, and price per square foot. Then answer the questions. Use these formulas:

Square feet = Length [times] Width

1 acre = 43,560 square feet

Lot 1: 460 feet wide, 340 feet long, $615,000

Square footage: _____

Acreage: _____

Price per square foot: _____

Lot 2: 320 feet wide, 480 feet long, $575,000

Square footage: _____

Acreage: _____

Price per square foot: _____

Lot 3: 400 feet wide, 575 feet long, $795,000

Square footage: _____

Acreage: _____

Price per square foot: _____

  1. Which lot is the largest? _____

  2. Which lot is the smallest? _____

  3. Which lot has the lowest per square foot price? _____

Chapter 9 Site Selection and Layout Planning

Academic Integration Activity

 **Social Studies**
Classifying

Directions In each series of terms, circle the one that does not belong. Then explain your choice on the line below.

1. Census tracts   Economic base   Financial incentives   Enterprise zones

_____

2. Type of business   Size of business

   Geographic barriers   Consumer price index

_____

3. Favorable zoning   Access to suppliers

   Access to transportation routes   Access to customers

_____

4. Newspaper ads   Contractors   Business contacts   Realtors

_____

5. Remodel   Build   Buy   Lease

_____

6. Map   Equipment list   Use of space design   Floor plan

_____

7. Access   Arrangement   Flow   Output

_____

8. Landscaping   Parking space   Traffic patterns   Fixtures

_____

9. Workstation   Worksite   Workbench   Workspace

_____

10. Facade   Signage   Entryways   Reception area

_____

Chapter 9 *Site Selection and Layout Planning* **113**

Chapter 9 Site Selection and Layout Planning

 **Test Prep**
Completion Tests

Directions Circle the letter of the word or phrase that best completes each of the following sentences.

1. The starting point in planning a layout for any facility is to _____.

   a. identify the activities that will take place
   b. define the objectives of the facility
   c. determine access, arrangement, and flow
   d. determine the space requirements for all activities

2. For a manufacturing operation, the primary physical layout consideration is the _____.

   a. placement of machinery
   b. delivery area
   c. storage area
   d. office space

3. For a wholesale operation, the primary physical layout consideration is _____.

   a. including sales showrooms
   b. providing cost-effective storage
   c. facilitating movement of productions in and out
   d. b and c

4. For a retail operation, the primary physical layout consideration is _____.

   a. attracting customers into the business
   b. providing the maximum number of sales stations
   c. the flow of customers through the business
   d. ease of exit

5. For a service operation, the primary physical layout consideration is the _____.

   a. appeal to customers
   b. ease of access
   c. service the business provides
   d. equipment and/or service area

6. For an extraction operation, the primary physical layout consideration is the _____.

   a. storage area
   b. sales office facility
   c. operations office facility
   d. environment in which the extraction occurs

7. Provisions for office space in layout plans is _____.

   a. important to some businesses but not others
   b. a necessity in every business
   c. the focal point of activity in every business
   d. essential for sales

8. Detailing of your business layout can _____.

   a. create an effective atmosphere
   b. enhance the company's image
   c. ensure safe and pleasant working conditions
   d. all of the above

9. In order to communicate your layout plans to those who will be implementing them, you should _____.

   a. verbalize them clearly
   b. commit them to paper
   c. identify close examples
   d. ask for recommendations

10. When locating a site for your business, you can identify potential sites and get an idea of the surroundings and suitability by using _____.

   a. structural soundness tests
   b. building evaluations
   c. visual surveys
   d. professional building inspectors

11. Machines and supporting activities are arranged along a product flow line in a _____.

   a. fixed product layout
   b. product layout
   c. process layout
   d. all of the above

12. Parts are brought to the job and workers come to the product in a _____.

   a. fixed product layout
   b. product layout
   c. process layout
   d. all of the above

13. Machines and equipment are grouped by function in a _____.

   a. fixed product layout
   b. product layout
   c. process layout
   d. all of the above

Chapter 9

Chapter 10 The Marketing Plan

 Note Taking

Directions As you read, write notes, facts, and main ideas in the note-taking column. Write key words and short phrases in the cues column. Then summarize the section in the summary box.

Cues	Note Taking
• marketing	**DEVELOPING A MARKETING PLAN** • Marketing is essential because success is determined in the marketplace. A marketing plan guides marketing activities to a desired conclusion.
• market research	**UPDATING THE MARKETING PLAN** • Ongoing market research is important because change is constant in business.
	Summary

Chapter 10

Chapter 10 The Marketing Plan
Section 10.1 Developing a Marketing Plan
Section Review: Critical Thinking

Directions Developing a creative, well-thought-out marketing plan is critical to the success of any business. It is particularly critical, however, to a small business serving the needs of a specific target market.

In the *BusinessWeek* Case Study for this chapter, you read about Hulu, a free, on-demand Web video service that is another example of how marketers are taking an increasingly savvy approach to capturing the Gen Y market. Below you will find a business description for Denim for All, a denim wear shop for males and females 16–24 years old. After reading the business description, answer the questions below and on the following pages. By doing so, you will be developing preliminary product and place strategies for this business, and designing marketing strategies for creating a buzz for Denim for All.

Business Description

Denim for All will be a denim wear shop for males and females, 16–24 years old, living within your county. Its product mix will consist of jeans, jackets, shirts, and other casual clothes in denim. The business might even expand to add tennis shoes, sweat suits, bib overalls, and denim jackets for young children.

The location of the business will be a leased space in a building a few miles outside of town. There are no other retailers there, and not much traffic, but there is plenty of parking and the rent is low. The hours operation will be 10 A.M.–5 P.M.

A. Product Decisions

As you develop the product strategy for this start-up business, answer the following questions. *Hint:* Keep the target market in mind as you decide on your answers.

1. Who is the target market for Denim for All? Is the target group too broad or too narrow? Explain.

_____

_____

_____

_____

_____

_____

_____

_____

Continued on next page

Chapter 10

2. What products should Denim for All sell? (Are there products proposed that should be eliminated? Could additional products enhance the product mix? Explain.)

_____

_____

_____

_____

3. How will the products offered by Denim for All be different from or better than the products offered by its competitors?

_____

_____

_____

_____

_____

4. How would you create a buzz for Denim for All?

_____

_____

_____

_____

B. Place Decisions

Place strategy involves how you will deliver your goods and services to your customers. Where will they buy? When will they buy? Will your product actually be available and ready for sale?

5. Is the location described appropriate for the business's target market(s)? Why or why not? If not, what would you propose as an alternate location?

_____

_____

_____

_____

_____

_____

Chapter 10

6. What would you propose for the physical layout of the business? Provide a brief description and explain how the layout will encourage sales. Then create a rough sketch on a separate sheet of paper.

_____

_____

_____

_____

_____

_____

7. From which channel members will the business obtain its products?

_____

_____

_____

_____

_____

8. Do the hours of operation match the times that the target market prefers to do business? Explain.

_____

_____

_____

_____

_____

9. What would you propose for the business's hours of operation? Explain how these hours would address the concerns of the target market.

_____

_____

_____

_____

_____

_____

Chapter 10

Chapter 10 The Marketing Plan

Section 10.2 Updating the Marketing Plan

Section Review: Analyze

Directions You should not assume that the target markets, customer demands, and competition you identify in starting up your business will always remain the same. Just ask the Big Bear sellers. Review the facts from the case below and help the bewildered bear bunch with their marketing planning.

Business Scenario

Business was great when we first started. As a hobby, my wife had been making monogrammed stuffed bears in different sporting gears. Then she began selling them to people to give as gifts. Pretty soon we had a little plant set up with employees, and we were selling to stores all over the state. It seemed that as long as we could turn out stuffed bears, people would buy them.

Then all of a sudden, sales took a nose dive. We had no idea why. Up until then, we had been doing most of our selling by sending catalogs to potential outlets. But with sales in such bad shape, I thought I had better get out on the road and call on our customers in person.

It did not take long to find out the problem. Almost every store I went into had sporting bears—different designs and shapes, but sporting bears just the same—made by someone else. On top of everything else, they were lower priced.

Well, we were able to get back some of our customers by giving bigger discounts, but it really cut into our profits. Now we have to figure out how to get the business back where it was. We are going to have to answer a lot of questions.

1. How can the bear makers find out what customers want now?

_____

_____

_____

_____

_____

_____

_____

_____

2. Should the product strategy be revised? If so, how?

_____

_____

_____

_____

_____

_____

_____

_____

_____

_____

_____

_____

_____

3. Could the owners find a better way to distribute the products? Explain.

_____

_____

_____

_____

_____

_____

_____

_____

_____

_____

_____

_____

_____

_____

_____

_____

Chapter 10

Chapter 10 The Marketing Plan

Software Activity
Word Processing Application

Directions The objective of this activity is to develop an outline for a marketing plan.

After entrepreneurs complete a market analysis and identify their target market, they are ready to take the next step in planning their new business. They must create an appropriate marketing plan. A marketing plan involves four basic strategies—product, place, price, and promotion. A fifth strategy, people, is often included. All of the strategies must be mixed appropriately for the plan to succeed.

On a separate piece of paper, prepare a brief outline of a marketing plan for a business you may be interested in starting in the future. Use the library, the Internet, or personal interviews to gather data. Present your basic strategies for each of the original four strategies of the marketing mix in an outline.

The headings for the outline have been completed for you and are shown below. Use the space provided at the bottom of the page to brainstorm. If you wish to use different information to start the outline, simply replace the headings with your own.

MARKETING PLAN

I. Product Strategy
II. Price Strategy
III. Promotion Strategy
IV. Place Strategy

_____
_____
_____
_____
_____
_____
_____
_____
_____
_____
_____
_____
_____

Chapter 10

Chapter 10 The Marketing Plan

Word Processing Directions

1. Start your spreadsheet software program.

2. Develop and write a brief outline for a marketing plan for the business that you have selected. Proofread and edit your work to make sure that it is correct and concise.

3. Save your work

4. Print out a copy of your completed job description if your teacher has instructed you to do so.

5. Answer the following questions.

Interpreting Results

1. What are examples of information that should be stated in the different parts of a marketing plan (product, price, promotion, and place)?

_____

_____

_____

_____

_____

_____

2. How should the entrepreneur evaluate the effectiveness of his/her marketing plan?

_____

_____

_____

_____

_____

Drawing Conclusions

3. Why must all four marketing strategies be mixed appropriately for a business to succeed?

_____

_____

_____

_____

Chapter 10 The Marketing Plan
Academic Integration Activity

English Language Arts
Writing Skills

Directions Listed below are seven factors to consider when developing the product strategy part of the marketing mix. Define the factors and write an example of each. The first one is completed for you.

1. Product features and benefits

   A product is made up of all the features, both physical and intangible, and benefits it offers to con-

   sumers. For example, convenience is a benefit.

   _____

   _____

   _____

2. Branding, packaging, and labeling

   _____

   _____

   _____

   _____

   _____

3. Product selection

   _____

   _____

   _____

   _____

   _____

   _____

Chapter 10

4. Product positioning

_____

_____

_____

_____

5. Product mix

_____

_____

_____

_____

_____

6. Questions about product decisions

_____

_____

_____

_____

7. Impact of technology on product strategy

_____

_____

_____

_____

_____

Chapter 10

Chapter 10 The Marketing Plan
Academic Integration Activity

Social Studies
Cause Marketing

Directions Read the article below about cause marketing. Then answer the questions.

CAUSE MARKETING

You see it on product labels and in advertisements almost every day: a business connecting itself to a charity organization, environmental group, or other good cause. This practice is part of *cause marketing,* a mutually beneficial arrangement between a for-profit business and a non-profit organization. Different from corporate giving (philanthropy), cause marketing is a strategic business action intended to improve a company's image and in turn entice consumers to buy their products or services.

One of the earliest and most notable cause marketing campaigns was in the 1970s between Famous Amos Cookies and the Literacy Volunteers of America. The cookie company founder, Wally Amos, became the national spokesperson for the literacy group, weaving in his company's story with the organization's expansion of literacy programs. The Famous Amos brand name became connected with an important cause, helping to sell a lot of cookies, but the effect was also good for Literacy Volunteers of America: the organization says that Wally Amos made more people aware of illiteracy in the U.S. than any other person in its history.

Other than the good feelings created by contributing to important social causes, the reason for-profit companies invest in cause marketing efforts is that it makes good business sense. The statistics back it up. According to a recent report by the Cone Millennial Cause Study, 89 percent of 13–25-year-olds said they would switch from one brand of a product to similar, comparatively priced product if the latter brand was associated with a "good cause." Another study reported that after the antacid company TUMS pledged to donate 10 cents from every bottle of TUMS sold to an organization funding fire departments across the U.S., the company saw a 16 percent increase in sales volume.

1. According to the article, how was the literacy cause brought to the attention of more Americans than it ever had in the past?

_____

_____

_____

_____

_____

Chapter 10

2. Why do you think TUMS' sales increased after it pledged to donate money from sales to help fund fire departments?

_____

_____

_____

_____

_____

_____

_____

_____

_____

_____

3. Think of your own cause marketing arrangement, using any real-life company and non-profit organization. Describe briefly a strategy for letting the public know about the arrangement.

_____

_____

_____

_____

_____

_____

_____

_____

_____

_____

_____

_____

Chapter 10

Chapter 10 The Marketing Plan
Case Study Activity
Advertising on Hulu

Directions Read the *BusinessWeek* Case Study feature in this chapter. Then read this case study and the questions on the next page.

Hulu Attracts Crowds but Not Ads
By Douglas MacMillan

Viewers can't get enough of Hulu, the joint venture from NBC Universal and News Corp. In a recent month it had the biggest surge in unique viewers of any online video site in that period.

But Hulu is facing plenty of roadblocks elsewhere, including among advertisers. At least one analyst says the site is struggling to find ads for many of its videos. And a lengthening list of rivals is rushing to move content online, spurred by the success of Hulu and online video leader YouTube, owned by Google. The speed bumps keep alive concerns over the ability to offset diminished demand for broadcast advertising with revenue from Internet programming.

Analysts are already revisiting their forecasts for ad spending on Hulu and other online video sites. Screen Digest's Arash Amel predicts Hulu will give YouTube a run for its money, but will generate $120 million in advertising this year, $60 million less than his original estimate. "What we've seen is rapid growth in consumption, but the advertising isn't keeping up," he says.

Based on Amel's studies of Hulu, the site has only sold about 60 percent of its ad inventory, with much of the remaining space filled with public service announcements. "We're still hugely optimistic about our ability to [make money from] the service," says Hulu spokeswoman Christina Lee, but it is "more challenging for us to project our future inventory accurately."

The payoff for advertisers is still far smaller online than with TV programming. A half-hour show that carries about two minutes of advertising on Hulu will have four times as much advertising when it is broadcast on TV. Although online ads can cost more per viewer, TV advertisers spend more because they can reach much larger audiences. Online video has the benefit of targeting certain types of customers and letting marketers include interactive elements, but in the current slow economy many advertisers are unwilling to experiment.

Rival online video offerings are finding success. Netflix has added more than a million subscribers since introducing streaming TV shows and movies to its service. "Being first doesn't always mean you'll be the longest-lasting or most successful company out there," says analyst Jason Blackwell. "[Hulu is] good for the industry because it's bringing awareness and finally creating momentum for these kinds of services, but at the same time it could become a victim of that success."

(Excerpted from *BusinessWeek.com* March 31, 2009)

Chapter 10

1. What are measures of Hulu's success as a marketing tool?

_____

_____

_____

2. What are signs that Hulu is not growing as rapidly as hoped?

_____

_____

_____

3. What is the benefit of online video to marketers? Why are advertisers slow to buy online ads on Hulu?

_____

_____

_____

_____

_____

4. Why do you think being the first to offer a particular service is not necessarily a good thing?

_____

_____

_____

_____

_____

5. If you have watched a television show or movie on Hulu or other online video service, describe the experience. Would you rather watch content online than on a television?

_____

_____

_____

_____

_____

Chapter 10

Chapter 10 The Marketing Plan

Test Prep
Using Flash Cards

Directions Create flash cards to help you remember concepts, facts, and figures. Write key words or answers to questions on the back of the cards. The first card is completed for you.

FRONT OF CARD (QUESTION)	BACK OF CARD (ANSWER)
Original Four Ps of marketing mix	product, place, price, promotion
Fifth and newest P of marketing	
What identifies a product	
Who are distribution intermediaries?	
What is a private brand?	
What is the process of investing in products or businesses with which you are not currently involved?	

Chapter 11 The Pricing Strategy

 Note Taking

Directions As you read, write notes, facts, and main ideas in the note-taking column. Write key words and short phrases in the cues column. Then summarize the section in the summary box.

Cues	Note Taking
	PRICE STRATEGY CONSIDERATION
• fixed	• Several factors influence setting a price for a good, service, or idea.
	CALCULATING AND CHANGING PRICES
• break-even point	• Break-even point is point at which gain from an economic activity equals the costs of doing it. Fixed Cost/Unit Selling Price – Variable Costs = Break-Even Point (Units)
	Summary

Chapter 11 The Pricing Strategy
Section 11.1 Price Strategy Consideration
Section Review: Evaluate

Directions This activity demonstrates some points to consider in setting a price for a new product: a newly designed piece of luggage. The case has wheels and a retractable handle for pulling. It is 14½ inches high and weighs only 9 pounds empty. This new model is approved as carry-on luggage for airline flights. It can be made of a heavy-duty polyester fabric or a Scotchguard™-treated tapestry fabric with leather trim.

1. **Determine the pricing objective.** Do you want to generate a certain sales volume, take away market share from competitors, or establish a prestigious or value-oriented image? How do you plan to do so?

   _____

   _____

   _____

   _____

   _____

   _____

   _____

2. **Study costs.** It costs $43.50 to make and market this piece of luggage. The company would like to get a return on investment on this new design of 10 to 20 percent. Determine the floor, midrange, and ceiling prices (plus 10, 15, 20 percent, respectively) that would be charged to retailers. Then, assuming that the retailers would charge customers at least double their cost, determine what the retail prices would be for this item.

   _____

   _____

   _____

   _____

   _____

   _____

   _____

3. **Estimate demand.** Who will be your final target market, and what will that group be willing to pay? This design is similar to the type of luggage flight attendants use. Research indicates that it is the luggage of choice for female business travelers and other people who do not like waiting for their luggage in airline terminals.

_____

_____

_____

_____

_____

4. **Study the competition.** With whom will you compete? Research indicates that the Verdi brand retails for $130, which means the price to the retailer is estimated to be between $50 and $65. The Destination brand retails for $99.99, which means the price to the retailer must have been between $40 and $50. Other competitors are somewhere between those two.

_____

_____

_____

_____

_____

_____

5. **Decide on an introduction strategy.** Will it be price skimming or penetration pricing? Why?

_____

_____

_____

_____

_____

_____

Chapter 11 The Pricing Strategy
Section 11.2 Calculating and Changing Prices
Section Review: Apply

Directions You are opening a new skateboard shop and everything is ready to go—everything except the merchandise, that is. It just arrived, and has to be priced and put out on the floor.

You have your invoice to work with, and you plan to use 100 percent markup on cost. To give the impression of bargain prices, you also plan to take one cent off the calculated price. You have everything you need, so get your calculator out and start figuring.

Item	Cost	Markup	Retail
Skateboard Brand A	$60.00		
Skateboard Brand B	$71.00		
Longboard	$85.00		
Trucks	$23.50		
Wheels	$17.25		
Pad Set	$16.00		
Helmet	$20.50		
Skate Tool	$6.00		

Six weeks later, some of the original shipment is still unsold. You decide on 20 percent as your initial markdown. Calculate the markdown on these items.

Item	Retail Price	Markdown	Sale Price
Skateboard Brand B			
Longboard			
Trucks			
Pad Set			
Skate Tool			

Two weeks after your first markdown, some items still remain. This time you plan to mark them down by 30 percent. Calculate the new sales price. If the price after markdown does not end in zero, round to the nearest zero before taking off one cent for the sale price.

Longboard			
Trucks			
Pad Set			
Skate Tool			

Another two weeks have gone by and you have to make room for more stock. This time you decide to mark down the unsold items by 50 percent. Do the calculations for these items.

Longboard			
Pad Set			
Skate Tool			

Chapter 11 The Pricing Strategy

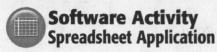

Software Activity
Spreadsheet Application

Directions The objective of this activity is to calculate cost, selling price, and markup for products.

One of the most important tasks facing entrepreneurs is establishing prices. The price must cover the firm's operating expenses while yielding the desired profit. The difference between selling price and the cost of the product is called the markup. Although it is important for entrepreneurs to know the dollar amount of a markup, it is usually more important to know the markup percentage. The Markup percentage is determined by dividing the dollar markup by the cost price. Usually, a firm's performance goals are presented in percentages. Percentages are usually much more meaningful when making comparisons.

The printout below shows 12 products sold by your firm. For some products you know the cost and desired markup and you must calculate selling price. For other products you know the planned selling price and you must calculate cost based on the desired markup. Finally, you will need to calculate the markup for some products when the cost and selling price are both known. For all products, you will need to calculate the markup percentage.

Item	Cost	Markup	Selling Price	Markup Percentage
1	$10.45	$10.49		
2	$72.16	$73.31		
3	$ .75	$ .71		
4	$4.35	$4.35		
5		$82.88	$166.00	
6		$12.58	$25.75	
7		$ .51	$1.00	
8		$2.56	$5.25	
9	$12.51		$25.00	
10	$2.34		$4.69	
11	$71.25		$142.99	
12	$ .25		$ .59	

Continued on next page

Spreadsheet Directions

1. Start your spreadsheet software program.

2. Re-create the table above using your spreadsheet program.

3. Calculate the following:
   - Find the selling price by adding cost and markup.
   - Find the cost by subtracting markup from selling price.
   - Find the markup by subtracting cost from selling price.
   - Find the markup percentage by dividing markup by cost.

4. After completing your calculations, save your work.

5. Print out a copy of your work if your teacher has instructed you to do so.

6. Answer the following questions.

Interpreting Results

1. Which product will have the highest markup? Which will have the lowest?

   _____

2. Which product will have the highest markup percentage? Which will have the lowest?

   _____

Drawing Conclusions

3. How will entrepreneurs typically mark products with the selling price calculated for items 1–4? Explain.

   _____

   _____

   _____

4. Will the products that have the highest markups necessarily produce the greatest profit for the entrepreneur?

   _____

   _____

   _____

5. What kind of impact will market prices have on the selling price an entrepreneur establishes for his/her products? Why?

   _____

   _____

   _____

Name _____ Date _____ Class _____

Chapter 11 The Pricing Strategy
Academic Integration Activity
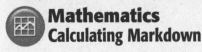
Mathematics
Calculating Markdown

Directions Read the scenario and study the table. Then answer the questions. Show your work.

Wendy Ballantine, owner of Heavy Lumber, is expecting a large shipment of prime Sitka spruce boards from Alaska in a few weeks. In order to make room for this in-demand wood, she is having a sale on her existing stock of oak, maple, fir and pine boards.

Product	Regular Selling Price (per board foot)	Markdown Percentage
Solid Oak	$2.15	10 percent
Red Oak	$4.99	20 percent
Maple, Grade 5A	$4.39	15 percent
Maple, Grade 3A	$1.99	32 percent
Fir	$3.50	23 percent
Pine	$0.89	44 percent

1. What is the sale price on red oak?

_____

_____

2. What is the sale price on pine?

_____

_____

3. What is the sale price on grade 3A maple?

_____

_____

4. Fred Essing, a building contractor, purchases 10 board feet of solid oak, 15 board feet of 3A maple, 12 board feet of 5A maple, and 20 board feet of fir. Find the total price Fred paid and the total markdown.

_____

_____

_____

_____

Chapter 11 The Pricing Strategy

Academic Integration Activity

 Science
The Price of Solar Energy

Directions Read the passage and the scenario. Then complete the table. Some of the information has been completed for you.

SOLAR AND WIND ENERGY

You may have read about power companies delivering electricity to customers from renewable solar and wind sources. How does this work?

The most common method used to convert sunlight into electricity is through the use of a device called a photovoltaic cell, also called a solar cell. In a photovoltaic solar panel, photons from sunlight knock electrons into a higher state of energy. This reaction creates electricity. For wind, tall turbines that look like gigantic propellers are turned by the wind. The turbine blades are connected to a magnet generator that creates power.

Consumers, environmentalists, and many governments see great potential in solar and wind power because these sources are renewable (they do not run out), non-polluting, and reduce greenhouse gas emissions. For example, while only 1.5 percent of the world's electricity usage currently comes from wind, the amount has more than tripled in the past decade. Wind accounts for approximately 19 percent of electricity production in Denmark, 11 percent in Spain and Portugal, and 7 percent in Germany and Ireland.

SD Electric offers a new program, Green Choice, for customers who want to get their electricity from renewable sources. With Green Choice, customers can select up to 100 percent of their power to come from solar, wind, or both. These customers will see an increase in their customer charge, which is normally $20.00, depending on how much solar and wind power they choose to buy. The markup for electricity from solar and wind is 15 percent. Complete the table for these SD Electric customers.

Customer	Percentage of Electricity Taken From			Customer Charge ($20.00 if 100% non-renewable)		
	Non-Renewable	Solar	Wind	Amount to Be Marked Up	Amount of Markup	Total Customer Charge
Eddie Oates	100%	0%	0%			$20.00
Kelly Mardin	20%	60%	20%	$16.00		
Chris Bond	50%	0%				
Steve Burdie		40%	60%			
Sara Edwards	0%	80%				

Chapter 11 The Pricing Strategy
Case Study Activity
Automotive Expenses

Directions Read the *BusinessWeek* Case Study feature in this chapter. Then study the graph and table. Use the information to answer the questions.

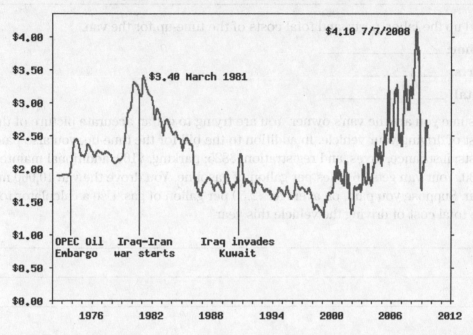

GAS PRICE HISTORY IN UNITED STATES
Regular Gasoline Price in Today's Dollars

Source: zFacts.com

THE COST OF A SINGLE SCHEDULED TUNE-UP FOR A FAMILY VAN

Description	Labor	Parts	Total
90,000 mile service	$295.40	$104.55	$399.95
Replace timing belt, water pump and accessory drive belts.	$687.50	$319.06	$1,006.56
During service, found side engine mount cracked. Replaced side engine mount.	$67.50	$63.95	$131.45
Replace spark plugs.	$0.00	$125.70	$125.70
Replace front brake pads, resurface front brake rotors.	$188.38	$61.57	$249.95
Perform power-steering fluid service.	$83.41	$6.54	$89.95
Hazardous waste removal	N/A	N/A	$5.00
Parts discount of 10%	N/A	N/A	($68.14)
Tax	N/A	N/A	$56.21
TOTAL	**$1,322.19**	**$681.37**	**$1,996.63**

Source: thedigeratilife.com

Continued on next page

1. In which year was the price of gas most expensive?

   _____

2. In approximately which year were gas prices least expensive?

   _____

3. From the information in the graph, what kinds of events create volatility in fuel prices?

   _____

   _____

4. Add up the labor, parts, and total costs of the tune-up for the van.

   Labor: _____

   Parts: _____

   Total: _____

5. Assume you are the van's owner. You are trying to get an accurate picture of the yearly cost of driving your vehicle. In addition to the bill for the tune-up, you also paid these costs: insurance, taxes, and registration, $825; parking, $160; additional maintenance, $230. Your van gets 16 miles per gallon of gasoline. You drove the van 10,000 miles this year. Suppose you paid, on average, $2.50 per gallon of gas. Use a calculator to compute the total cost of driving the vehicle this year.

   _____

   _____

   _____

   _____

   _____

   _____

   _____

   _____

   _____

   _____

   _____

   _____

   _____

Chapter 11 The Pricing Strategy

Test Prep
True-False Tests

Directions Take the practice test below. Circle T for true or F for false. Rewrite false statements so that they are true.

1. Psychological pricing, prestige pricing, and price lining are all promotional pricing techniques.   **T F**

   _____

   _____

   _____

2. Odd/even pricing uses odd prices ($39.95) to suggest higher quality and even prices ($40.00) to suggest bargains.   **T F**

   _____

   _____

   _____

3. Price skimming involves charging a high initial price for new products to recover cost or maximize profits as soon as possible.   **T F**

   _____

   _____

   _____

4. Penetration pricing attempts to build sales volume by charging lower initial prices.   **T F**

   _____

   _____

   _____

5. Break-even point occurs when sales equal costs minus the expenses of making or distributing a product.   **T F**

   _____

   _____

   _____

Chapter 12 The Promotion Strategy

 Note Taking

Directions As you read, write notes, facts, and main ideas in the note-taking column. Write key words and short phrases in the cues column. Then summarize the section in the summary box.

Cues	Note Taking
	DEVELOPING A PROMOTION STRATEGY
• image	• Promotion: communication intended to persuade, inform, or remind a target market about its business or products.
	BUDGETING AND IMPLEMENTING PROMOTIONAL PLANS
• industry average: standard used to compare costs	• Established businesses use previous plans and sales figures to help develop promotional budget. New businesses must gather information and estimate expenses.
Summary	

Chapter 12 The Promotion Strategy
Section 12.1 Developing a Promotion Strategy
Section Review: Planning

Directions The director of a local theater company has just learned that you are becoming an expert in the development and management of small business ventures—specifically, the development and implementation of promotional plans. And has she got a deal for you!

The company is doing a production of a holiday pageant. It will be on the weekends during December. Performances will be held on Friday and Saturday evenings, with special children's matinees on Saturday afternoons. The children's performances will include refreshments and chaperones, so parents can drop off the kids for a few hours while they do their holiday shopping.

Your mission is to develop a great promotional plan for the children's performances. Use the following questions to develop your ideas.

Planning

1. Who is your target market(s)?

   _____

   _____

   _____

2. Why should you refocus on your target market before selecting your promotional activities?

   _____

   _____

   _____

3. What is the theme you will present or the image that will guide your promotional efforts?

   _____

   _____

   _____

4. When will you begin to implement your promotional plan?

   _____

   _____

   _____

Continued on next page

Selecting Your Promotional Mix

5. Based on your product (special matinees for children) and your market, which promotional channel(s) will you use? Explain.

_____

_____

_____

6. Which element of the promotional mix will you use most? Why? What specific strategies will you use? Why?

_____

_____

_____

Publicity

On a separate sheet of paper, develop a publicity release for the local newspaper. Use your creativity. Be sure to answer the following: Who? What? When? Where? Why?

Advertising

Assuming that you selected radio as a medium in the advertising element of your promotional mix—and even if you did not—develop a 30-second radio ad and prepare to present it to the class. To construct a successful radio ad, you should do the following:

- Grab the listener's attention, not only with the words but with the sound and music as well. Describe how you would use sound effects and/or music.
- Tell immediately about the benefit of the product.
- Be sure to mention the name of the product often.
- Be positive, keep it simple, and speak in a conversational style.

Sales Promotion

Sales promotion involves the use of incentives or interest-building activities to stimulate traffic or sales. On a separate sheet of paper, design a promotion to stimulate the sale of matinee tickets. In your description, be sure to include the type of promotion, a description, and your rationale as to why it will be effective. Be creative and provide as much detail as you can.

Chapter 12 The Promotion Strategy
Section 12.2 Budgeting and Implementing Promotional Plans

Section Review: Decision Making

Directions When trying to get the most for your advertising dollar, you should not always rely on obvious or readily available figures. For example, the Web site with the largest number of hits is not necessarily your best choice. Neither is the newspaper, radio or television station with the lowest cost per ad. What you need to look at is the cost of reaching *your particular customers*.

The following examples will guide you through the steps in this calculation. Generally, you must determine what portion of the particular medium's audience or circulation your customers represent and then divide the cost of the ad by this figure.

1. You are trying to decide between two social-networking Web sites to advertise your product. PeoplePlace.net has 200,000 unique visitors per month and charges $3,500 for a banner ad. FriendCentral.com has 180,000 unique visitors per month and charges $3,800 for the same ad. From your research you estimate that 30 percent of PeoplePlace users and 42 percent of FriendCentral users are potential buyers of your product. Determine which Web site offers the lowest cost per potential customer.

	PeoplePlace	**FriendCentral**
Unique visitors		
Percentage of potential customers reached		
Number of potential customers reached		
Cost of ad		
Cost of ad per user		
Cost of ad per potential customer reached		
Web site with the lower cost per reader (check one)		
Web site with the lower cost per potential customer (check one)		

Conclusion:

_____

_____

_____

Continued on next page

2. You are trying to decide in which of two trade publications to advertise your company. *Business Monthly* magazine has a circulation of 100,000 and charges $3,500 for a half-page ad. The *Index Report* has a circulation of 125,000 and charges $3,000 for the same space. From your analysis of their readership, you estimate that 25 percent of *Business Monthly* readers are potential clients and 20 percent of the *Index Report's*. Determine which publication offers the lower cost per potential client.

	Business Monthly	Index Report
Circulation		
Percentage of potential customers reached		
Number of potential customers reached		
Magazine that reaches the largest number of readers		
Magazine that reaches the largest number of potential clients		
Cost of ad		
Cost of ad per reader		
Cost of ad per potential customer reached		
Magazine with the lower cost per reader (check one)		
Magazine with the lower cost per potential client (check one)		

Conclusion:

_____

_____

_____

_____

_____

_____

Chapter 12

Chapter 12 The Promotion Strategy

Software Activity
Database Application

Directions The objective of this activity is to estimate percentage of net sales to be spent.

You own an advertising agency representing many different types of retailers. Many of these clients are new entrepreneurs who have not been in business for very long. Part of your duties involves helping the store managers in developing a promotional plan. One component of that plan is to determine a budget for all promotional activities. For this purpose, you have developed a database using industry averages on the percentage of sales spent on advertising. You have constructed the database so that you can assist various types of retailers, both large and small.

PERCENTAGE OF SALES SPENT ON ADVERTISING

Total Assets	$10,000–$249,000	$250,000–$499,999	$500,000–$999,999	Over $1,000,000
Category of Business				
Apparel	2.22	2.53	2.59	1.45
Building Materials and Supplies	--	1.28	1.11	0.82
Computer Stores	--	--	--	1.27
Florists	1.68	1.91	--	--
Grocery	0.45	0.27	0.18	0.81
Furniture/Appliances	--	3.12	2.75	3.12
General Merchandise	2.56	2.12	1.97	0.60
Gift Shops	1.35	1.35	1.89	--
Jewelry	1.69	2.63	2.84	1.60
Office Supplies	0.87	1.23	1.28	1.05
Shoes	3.30	1.58	1.01	--
Sporting Goods	2.05	1.72	2.02	1.72
Electronics	1.76	1.53	2.21	--
Automobiles	--	0.30	0.84	0.51
DVD and Video Game Rentals	3.10	2.46	--	--

Continued on next page

Database Directions

1. Start your database software program.

2. Re-create the table from the previous page using your database program.

3. Perform the sort function on the data in the four categories of assets.

4. Save your sorted databases.

5. Print out a copy of your work if your teacher has instructed you to do so.

6. Answer the following questions.

Interpreting Results

1. How many types of the firms with total assets of $10,000–$249,000 spent over 1.5 percent of their sales on advertising? Which category of business spent the largest percentage? Which spent the smallest percentage?

_____

_____

_____

2. By examining the results of all four sorts, determine who spent the largest and smallest percentage of their sales on advertising.

_____

_____

_____

Drawing Conclusions

3. What reasons could you give for some data not being available?

_____

_____

_____

4. Based on the information collected, would you recommend to the owner of a sporting goods store to spend exactly 2.05 percent of sales on advertising?

_____

_____

_____

Chapter 12

Chapter 12 The Promotion Strategy
Academic Integration Activity

Mathematics
Reading Tables

Directions The table below lists the amount of money spent on network television advertising over a recent three-year period. Read the table, then answer the questions.

SPENDING ON NETWORK TELEVISION ADVERTISING
(in millions of U.S. dollars)

Type of Product	Year 1	Year 2	Year 3
Apparel and footwear	$370	$341	$286
Automotive products	2,258	1,994	1,865
Candy and soft drinks	715	726	772
Computers	239	258	312
Department and discount stores	469	432	390
Food and food products	1,305	1,269	1,298
Household items	527	498	510
Insurance	237	332	368
Laundry soaps, cleansers, and polishers	212	301	280
Medicines	1,438	1,631	1,802
Motion pictures	805	862	903
Pets and pet products	97	121	111
Toiletries, cosmetics, and hair care	1,182	1,200	1,165
Toys and games	293	268	255
Travel, hotels, and resorts	182	204	190

1. On which types of products did the amount spent on advertising decrease each year?

   _____

   _____

2. On which types of products did the amount spent on advertising increase each year?

   _____

   _____

3. On which type of product was the most spent in all three years?

   _____

   _____

4. What was the total amount spent on all products in each year?

   Year 1: _____   Year 2: _____   Year 3: _____

Chapter 12

Chapter 12 The Promotion Strategy
Academic Integration Activity

Social Studies
Television Advertising

Directions Read the article about television advertising, then answer the questions.

DODGERS VS. PHILLIES

The first television advertisement aired on July 1, 1941, before a baseball game between the Brooklyn Dodgers and Philadelphia Phillies. The commercial was aired on a New York City television station. The Bulova Watch Company paid $9 to air a 20-second ad. At the time, only a few thousand American households had a television. Most people had never seen one.

Since then, TV ads have become hugely influential on American culture and on cultures around the world. They have shaped the way we dress, what we eat and drink, what we drive, even the prescription medicines we take. As we age, our memories of childhood often include our favorite TV ads and commercial characters and catchphrases. No wonder: the American Psychological Association estimated that the average child views 40,000 TV ads per year and that children influence $670 billion worth of parental spending annually.

Sources: Oracle Education Foundation, American Psychological Association, TNS Media Intelligence/CMAG

---

1. How much did the first television ad cost to air? _____

2. Who bought the ad? _____

3. How much parental spending each year is influenced by children?
   _____

4. Watching television at home, use a timekeeping device, pen, and paper to keep track of the ads you see for one hour. Write down the following for each ad: length in seconds, type of ad (product, commercial service, or public service), and what is being advertised. Which ad did you find most effective? What was effective about it?

   _____

   _____

   _____

   _____

   _____

   _____

   _____

   _____

Chapter 12 The Promotion Strategy
Case Study Activity
Video Game Consumers

Directions Read the *BusinessWeek* Case Study feature in this chapter. Then use the information below to complete the activity.

Industry Facts About the Entertainment Software Industry

America's entertainment software industry creates a wide variety of computer and video games to meet the demands and tastes of audiences as diverse as our nation's population. Today's gamers include millions of Americans of all ages and backgrounds. In fact, more than two-thirds of all American households play games. This vast audience is fueling the growth of this multi-billion dollar industry and bringing jobs to communities across the nation. Below is a list of the top 10 entertainment software industry facts:

1. In the most recent year for which data is available, U.S. computer and video game software sales grew 22.9 percent to $11.7 billion—more than quadrupling industry software sales since 1996.

2. 68 percent of American households play computer or video games.

3. The average game player is 35 years old and has been playing games for 12 years.

4. The average age of the most frequent game purchaser is 39 years old.

5. 40 percent of all game players are women. In fact, women over the age of 18 represent a significantly greater portion of the game-playing population (34 percent) than boys age 17 or younger (18 percent).

6. In a recent year, 25 percent of Americans over the age of 50 played video games, an increase from nine percent in 1999.

7. 37 percent of heads of households play games on a wireless device, such as a cell phone or PDA, up from 20 percent in 2002.

8. 84 percent of all games sold in 2008 were rated "E" for Everyone, "T" for Teen, or "E10+" for Everyone 10+.

9. 92 percent of game players under the age of 18 report that their parents are present when they purchase or rent games.

10. 63 percent of parents believe games are a positive part of their children's lives.

Continued on next page

1. Do you play computer or video games in your home? Have you or someone in your family purchased at least one game in the past year?

_____

_____

2. If you play video games, how long have you been playing?

_____

_____

3. What elements of the promotion mix have you seen for computer and video games? Describe them.

_____

_____

_____

_____

_____

4. If you play video games, list some of the companies that make the games you play. Describe characteristics of these companies' products that make them attractive.

_____

_____

_____

5. The "10 Facts" listed on the previous page come from an article published by the Entertainment Software Association, a group that works to promote the interests of the gaming industry. What purpose does the article serve in promoting this industry?

_____

_____

_____

_____

_____

_____

_____

Chapter 12 The Promotion Strategy

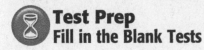 **Test Prep**
Fill in the Blank Tests

Directions Take the practice test below. Complete the sentences with content vocabulary.

1. The placement of newsworthy items about a company or product in the media is/are _____.

2. Exhibits placed in showrooms, at points-of-purchase and outside businesses to increase buyer awareness is/are _____.

3. Something of value that a customer receives in addition to the good or service being purchased is a(n) _____.

4. Games used by businesses to draw attention to what the company has to offer is/are _____.

5. Returning part of the purchase price to customers is a sales promotion technique called a(n) _____.

6. Oral presentations to one or more potential buyers with the intent of making a sale is/are _____.

7. Activities designed to create goodwill toward a business, often reported by the media, are _____.

8. A company that, in its role as intermediary between a business and the media, communicates a message to a target audience is called a(n) _____.

9. When a panel of viewers evaluate an ad before it runs, giving reactions and perceptions, the procedure is called a(n) _____.

10. The personality and impression people get from a company is that company's _____.

11. A series of related promotional activities with a similar theme is called a(n) _____.

12. Giveaways such as pens, caps, and company-branded T-shirts are promotional items called _____.

Chapter 13 The Promotion Strategy: Developing and Managing Sales

 Note Taking

Directions As you read, write notes, facts, and main ideas in the note-taking column. Write key words and short phrases in the cues column. Then summarize the section in the summary box.

Cues	Note Taking
• personal selling	**ORGANIZING AND PREPARING A SALES FORCE** • Personal selling is a direct presentation to help a prospect, or potential customer, make a buying decision.
• sales planning	**PLANNING, DIRECTING, AND EVALUATING SALES** • Sales planning involves making sales forecasts, budgeting sales, establishing territories and setting quotas (performance goals).
Summary	

Chapter 13 The Promotion Strategy: Developing and Managing Sales

Section 13.1 Organizing and Preparing a Sales Force

Section Review: Apply

Directions School Scene, your school spirit-wear distribution company, was organized to sell jackets, school sweatshirts, T-shirts, caps, and similar items to school stores. Business has been solid. But, like many business people, you are always on the lookout for new product to add to your line.

You think you may have found a winner. Blue Collar brand work clothes are beginning to appear in the high schools where your sales reps sell. You have contacted the manufacturer, and they are interested in having you represent them in the market.

Two problems, though. One, they want you to agree to increase the number of school stores you sell to before they sign on. Two, your sales staff has no background in selling this line. Both problems can be resolved. The first may be solved by additional prospecting, and the second, by providing training in selling the product line to your sales force.

Answer the following questions as a starting point for your prospecting and training.

A. Expanding Your Accounts

1. How can you find out where to reach additional school stores? Can you find a way to narrow your list down to those with a high potential for buying?

   _____

   _____

   _____

   _____

   _____

2. How can you get background information about the prospects that would help your sales efforts? What kind of questions would you like to have answered?

   _____

   _____

   _____

   _____

   _____

Continued on next page

Chapter 13

B. Developing a Sales Training Model Presentation

3. How would you approach your existing customers about the new product line? What sales approach would you use with new customers?

_____

_____

_____

_____

4. What questions would you ask to determine their awareness of the trend? What questions would you ask to determine their perceived need for the product line?

_____

_____

_____

_____

5. How would you organize your presentation of the product line? What benefits would you emphasize? How would you get the buying team (and/or the store adviser) involved with the product during the presentation?

_____

_____

_____

_____

_____

6. What objections would you expect? List all you can think of. What technique would you use for overcoming each objection? (Give an example of how you would use each technique.)

_____

_____

_____

_____

7. What techniques would you use to close the sale?

_____

_____

_____

_____

_____

8. You are presenting a whole line of work clothes. What kinds of items might you use for suggestion selling for building your sale?

_____

_____

_____

_____

_____

_____

9. What information would you have to obtain when writing up the order in this situation? Note: It may be useful to make a mock-up of an order form.

_____

_____

_____

_____

10. When would you do your follow-up for the sale? What questions would you ask? What kinds of problems might you run into? What would you do to address the problems? How would you handle the customer's dissatisfaction if there was any?

_____

_____

_____

_____

_____

_____

Chapter 13 The Promotion Strategy: Developing and Managing Sales

Section 13.2 Planning, Directing, and Evaluating Sales

Section Review: Explain

Directions In Chapter 13, you learned about four different techniques for supervising your sales force—personal contacts, sales reports, electronic communications, and meetings. For each of the following situations, write the primary technique(s) you would use on the line to the left. Then give brief details and rationale in the space following the situation.

1. _____ One of your new salespeople is very productive in terms of calls made and new prospects contacted. However, she is making very few sales.

_____

_____

_____

2. _____ Your most recent sales contest was very competitive and resulted in a hefty increase in volume for all of your salespeople. Now that it is over, sales are trailing off across the board.

_____

_____

_____

3. _____ For the past year, sales have been going up at a steady rate. Unfortunately, sales expenses have been going up nearly twice as fast.

_____

_____

_____

4. _____ The performance of your top salesperson has declined greatly during the last quarter. You have heard that he is working a second job to pay for his wife's large medical expenses.

_____

_____

_____

Chapter 13

5. _____ The information submitted on a sales-call report from one of your salespeople is totally out of line with the results that were obtained.

_____

_____

_____

6. _____ You have new product information to disseminate that requires detailed explanation. Due to schedule conflicts, you will not be able to bring the sales force together anytime soon.

_____

_____

_____

7. _____ Your top competitor has moved ahead of you in sales in each of your territories. You need input regarding the causes from your salespeople immediately.

_____

_____

_____

8. _____ You are adding a new product line. Proper training in the technical aspects of the products, as well as their features and benefits, will require considerable time.

_____

_____

_____

9. _____ One of your salespeople who used to struggle with quotas has increased her sales volume dramatically. It appears, however, that she has not been following the policy of checking with production before committing to delivery dates. They cannot fill the orders on time.

_____

_____

_____

Chapter 13

Chapter 13 The Promotion Strategy: Developing and Managing Sales

Software Activity
Database Application

Directions The objective of this activity is to analyze sales output of employees.

You own a wholesale distribution center, supplying products to department and sporting goods stores in three states. As the owner of the firm, one of your responsibilities is to evaluate the performance of your sales staff. This evaluation will allow you to determine the effectiveness of your marketing plan and your operations.

On the printout below you will find employee sales data from last week. The database contains information on the amount of sales, type of retail business making the purchase, and the location (city and state) of those clients.

Salesperson	Dollar Sales	Type of Store	City	State
1	$5,000	Department	Asheville	NC
1	$1,500	Department	Hendersonville	NC
1	$1,000	Sporting Goods	Boone	NC
1	$4,200	Department	Knoxville	TN
2	$6,000	Department	Charlotte	NC
2	$5,220	Department	Charlotte	NC
2	$1,250	Sporting Goods	Salisbury	NC
2	$750	Sporting Goods	Gastonia	NC
3	$650	Sporting Goods	Shelby	NC
3	$1,430	Sporting Goods	Greenville	SC
3	$980	Sporting Goods	Spartanburg	SC
3	$1,110	Sporting Goods	Greenville	SC

Chapter 13

Database Directions

1. Start your database software program.

2. Re-create the table from the previous page using your database program.

3. Perform the sort function on the following data:

   - sort by dollar sales
   - sort the data by type of store
   - sort the data by state

4. Save your work after performing each sort.

5. Print out a copy of your work if your teacher has instructed you to do so.

6. Answer the following questions.

Interpreting Results

1. Which salesperson made the largest single sale?

   _____

2. Which type of store accounts for most of the sales made?

   _____

3. Which state accounted for most sales made?

   _____

Drawing Conclusions

4. You want to increase your employees' sales volumes. On which type of store would you suggest for them to focus in order to reach this goal? Explain.

   _____

   _____

   _____

5. How could you use the location data to develop future plans for your firm?

   _____

   _____

   _____

   _____

Chapter 13

Chapter 13 The Promotion Strategy: Developing and Managing Sales

Academic Integration Activity

 English Language Arts
Reading Skills

Directions Place a check mark (√) under one of the columns to indicate whether the consumer has a rational buying motive or an emotional buying motive for making a purchase. The first one is completed for you.

Motive	Rational	Emotional
I'm not sure if this is the right camping tent, but this store has a generous return policy.	√	
I needed eggs and milk, and this store was right by my house.		
All of my friends think this designer brand is the coolest.		
This expensive watch suggests that I am a person with wealth and style.		
These tools are built to last.		
Driving Ford trucks is a family tradition.		
We like this organic peanut butter because it has no additives or preservatives.		
I'm in a hurry, so the drive-thru at Burgerville is a good option for grabbing a quick meal.		
This big, powerful SUV makes me feel invincible on the road.		
This brand of washing machine has a reputation for almost never breaking down.		
Typically these gourmet cookies are too expensive for our budget, but this 2-for-1 sale is too good to pass up.		
I don't usually buy downloads of this kind of music, but I have great memories of hearing this song when I was a kid.		
Volvos get consistently high ratings in crash-safety tests.		
These shoes are very comfortable.		

Chapter 13 The Promotion Strategy: Developing and Managing Sales

Academic Integration Activity

Social Studies
Sales Employment Data

Directions The United States Bureau of Labor Statistics is a valuable resource for career research. The bureau's Web site gives access to information about specific job categories, including descriptions of the work, qualifications, average pay, and anticipated employment growth.

Follow the instructions to access the bureau's Web site and access information about a career as a sales representative. Use your research to answer the questions.

- Use a search engine to find the Web site for the United States Bureau of Labor Statistics.
- Use the Web site's search engine to locate the Occupational Outlook Handbook entry for Sales Representative, Wholesale and Manufacturing.

1. What is the typical educational level of a sales representative?

_____

_____

_____

_____

_____

_____

2. About how many people are employed as sales representatives? What percentage worked in wholesale trade?

_____

_____

_____

_____

_____

_____

Continued on next page

3. What is the job outlook for sales representatives? Describe the employment change and job prospects.

_____

_____

_____

_____

_____

_____

_____

4. What are the median annual earnings of sales representatives, including commissions? What do the highest 10 percent earn? In which industry do sales representatives earn the highest incomes?

_____

_____

_____

_____

_____

_____

_____

_____

_____

_____

_____

5. Why do you think educational level is not a barrier to working in the sales field?

_____

_____

_____

_____

_____

_____

_____

_____

_____

_____

Chapter 13 The Promotion Strategy: Developing and Managing Sales

Case Study Activity

Calculating Commission

Directions Read the *BusinessWeek* Case Study feature in this chapter. Then read the scenario. Use the information to complete the chart and answer questions.

Assume you are a payroll clerk for V12 Group. V12 representatives work on straight commission. As you read in the Case Study, since V12 founder Paul Chachko hired Jeff Berke to lead the sales team, changes have been made in the company's commission system. The flat 5.5% commission has been eliminated—if reps do not make quota, their commission is 5%. If they make quota, total commission ranges from 6% up to 10% if quotas are doubled.

The chart below shows the yearly sales performance of eight V12 reps. Use the following guidelines to complete the chart. Some of the information is filled in for you.

Quota: $800,000
Commission for sales between:
　　$800,000 and $1.149 million—6%
　　$1.15 million and $1.299 million—7%
　　$1.3 million and $1.449 million—8%
　　$1.45 million and $1.599 million—9%
　　$1.6 million and up—10%

Representative	Gross Sales	Commission %	Commission Amount
S. Koysin	$ 937,248	6	$ 56,234.88
M. Ward	1,365,369	8	
J. Khan	1,772,495		
A. Johnson	733,027		
F. Aldridge	1,152,705		
L. Choo	1,586,318		
R. Smith	810,268		
B. Haynie	2,004,100		

1. How many of the reps made their yearly sales quota?

_____

2. Who, if anyone, doubled their quota?

_____

3. How much less would B. Haynie have made under V12's previous flat commission system?

_____

_____

Chapter 13 The Promotion Strategy: Developing and Managing Sales

Test Prep
Unmatching

Directions Take the practice test below. In each series of terms, circle the one that does not belong. Then explain your choice on the line below.

1. personal selling   sales promotion   consumer research   publicity

_____

_____

_____

2. sales staff   sales organization   sales force   salespeople

_____

_____

_____

3. full sales representation   routine sales situations   high level assistance
extensive product knowledge

_____

_____

_____

4. features   potential satisfaction   advantages   possible uses

_____

_____

_____

5. social approval   power   affection   dependability

_____

_____

_____

6. attention   interest   determination   action

_____

_____

7. soliciting referrals   checking public records   improving products
cold canvassing

_____

_____

8. competitors' records   industry information   customer surveys
sales records

_____

_____

9. provide sales incentives   summarize sales results
indicate weakness in sales preparation   control selling expenses

_____

_____

10. orders taken   miles traveled   new accounts sold
sales meetings attended

_____

_____

11. industry sales analysis   analysis of sales volume   marketing cost analysis
individual sales performance analysis

_____

_____

_____

Chapter 13

Chapter 14 Preparing and Planning to Manage

 Note Taking

Directions As you read, write notes, facts, and main ideas in the note-taking column. Write key words and short phrases in the cues column. Then summarize the section in the summary box.

Cues	Note Taking
	ENTREPRENEUR OR MANAGER?
• manager	• Business owners rely on others for assistance in reaching a common goal.
• situational management: using whatever management style a situation dictates	**MANAGEMENT STYLES AND SKILLS** • Management style: manner in which management responsibilities are approached
Summary	

Chapter 14 Preparing and Planning to Manage
Section 14.1 Entrepreneur or Manager?
Section Review: Apply

Directions This story is, in a way, an example of management at its best and its worst in a particular situation. While it is obviously not a business story, you will be applying some of the key points from Chapter 14 to assess the captain's management style and effectiveness.

Below and on the next page are questions about this story. Be sure to relate each response to actual business management as it was discussed in the chapter.

BATTLESHIP

Two battleships assigned to the training squadron had been at sea on maneuvers in heavy weather for several days. I was serving on the lead battleship and was on watch on the bridge as night fell. The visibility was poor with patchy fog, so the captain remained on the bridge keeping an eye on all activities.

Shortly after dark, the lookout on the wing of the bridge reported, "Light, bearing on the starboard bow."

"Is it steady or moving astern?" the captain called out.

Lookout replied, "Steady, captain," which meant we were on a dangerous collision course with that ship.

The captain then called to the signalman, "Signal that ship: We are on a collision course and advise you change course 20 degrees."

Back came a signal, "Advisable for you to change course 20 degrees."

The captain said, "Send: I'm a captain, change course 20 degrees."

"I'm a seaman second class," came the reply. "You had better change course 20 degrees."

By that time, the captain was furious. He spat out, "Send: I'm a battleship. Change course 20 degrees."

Back came the flashing light, "I'm a lighthouse."

We changed course.

Continued on next page

Chapter 14

1. Using the four management functions (planning, organizing, directing, and controlling), explain how the captain of the battleship was an effective manager.

a. **Planning**

_____

_____

_____

_____

_____

b. **Organizing**

_____

_____

_____

_____

_____

c. **Directing**

_____

_____

_____

_____

_____

d. **Controlling**

_____

_____

_____

_____

_____

_____

_____

Chapter 14

Chapter 14 Preparing and Planning to Manage
Section 14.2 Management Styles and Skills
Section Review: Time Management

Directions How well do you manage your time? How often do you hear someone say, "I really want to do that, but I don't have any time." Are you one of those people? The test is to see how you spend your time. Find out if you are spending it doing the things that will help you get where you want to go. That is really all that time management is: managing time so you can achieve what you want to achieve (even if all you want is to sleep in on Saturday morning). Use the charts on the next pages to evaluate your time management skills.

Activity 1 First, ask yourself how you spend your time. Use Chart 1 on page 172 to record how many hours a day you think you spend on a given activity. Some categories of activities are listed for you. Use an additional sheet of paper if you have more activities to list than there is room for in each box. (You can design your own grid if you wish.) Complete this first chart before moving on to the next activity.

Activity 2 Now you have a chart of how you think you spend your time. But wait! Does it represent the best use you can make of your time? Think—how would you spend your time if you wanted to do your best to accomplish your goals? Summarize your conclusions by filling in Chart 2 on page 173. (Note: You may need to take a few minutes to consider what your goals are before you begin—educational, social, personal, career, and so on.) Complete this second chart before moving on to the next activity.

Activity 3 Now it is time to find out how you actually spend your time. For one week, keep a daily record of every activity you engage in and the amount of time you spend on it. At the end of each day, summarize your data by making appropriate entries in Chart 3 on page 174.

Activity 4 At week's end, you will have three charts—one showing how you think you spend your time, another showing how you could most effectively spend your time, and a third showing how you actually spend your time. When you have these three charts completed, you will be ready to answer the questions that begin on page 175.

Chapter 14

Chapter 14 Preparing and Planning to Manage

Chart 1—How You Think You Spend Your Time

	Sun.	Mon.	Tue.	Wed.	Thurs.	Fri.	Sat.
Sleeping							
Eating							
Classes							
Homework							
Hygiene							
Athletics							
Daydreaming							
Social time							
Bus/car/subway rides							
Shopping							
Chores							
Leisure							
Religious activities							
Other activities							

Chart 2—How You Could Spend Your Time Most Effectively

	Sun.	Mon.	Tue.	Wed.	Thurs.	Fri.	Sat.
Sleeping							
Eating							
Classes							
Homework							
Hygiene							
Athletics							
Daydreaming							
Social time							
Bus/car/subway rides							
Shopping							
Chores							
Leisure							
Religious activities							
Other activities							

Chapter 14

Continued on next page

Chart 3—How You Actually Spend Your Time

	Sun.	Mon.	Tue.	Wed.	Thurs.	Fri.	Sat.
Sleeping							
Eating							
Classes							
Homework							
Hygiene							
Athletics							
Daydreaming							
Social time							
Bus/car/subway rides							
Shopping							
Chores							
Leisure							
Religious activities							
Other activities							

Chapter 14

1. After comparing the three charts, what new discovery have you made about the way you spend your time?

_____

_____

_____

_____

_____

2. What are the major differences between how you think you spend your time (Chart 1) and how you actually spend it (Chart 3)?

_____

_____

_____

_____

_____

3. What are the major differences between how you believe you should spend your time (Chart 2) and how you actually spend it (Chart 3)?

_____

_____

_____

_____

_____

4. What changes will you need to make in your schedule in order to make more time for the activities in Chart 2?

_____

_____

_____

_____

_____

Chapter 14

Continued on next page

5. Do you believe you are managing your time well? If not, what short-and long-term goals do you think could help you manage your time better? If you are managing your time well, are there changes you might make to fine-tune your use of time? If so, describe them.

_____

_____

_____

_____

6. In the chapter section titled Developing Management Skills, there are seven skills that are needed to carry out management activities successfully. Think back to the story of the captain in the previous section activity. Choose three of these management skills, and show how the captain was effective or ineffective in using them.

a. Skill

_____

_____

_____

_____

_____

b. Skill

_____

_____

_____

_____

_____

c. Skill

_____

_____

_____

_____

_____

Chapter 14

Chapter 14 Preparing and Planning to Manage

Software Activity
Word Processing Application

Directions The objective of this activity is to write an employee policy.

Directing is a key management function that entrepreneurs must perform. It involves conveying plans, assignments, and instructions to employees. This also includes writing policies for the staff. Employee policies should communicate an entrepreneur's goals and expectations to employees while motivating them to perform their best.

Policies can make it clear to employees what kind of behavior is expected in the workplace. They can set clear guidelines on what is and is not appropriate. Policies can help entrepreneurs avoid, or at least defend against, lawsuits. Policies should be clearly and concisely written, and should state specific consequences that would result when they are not followed.

Practice Situation

You need to develop and write a policy to deal with employee tardiness. Your desire is to make sure that employees are punctual; however, you also want the policy to be flexible. A suggested opening has been included to get you started (see below). If you wish to alter the opening, simply replace the one provided with your own.

EMPLOYEE POLICY—PUNCTUALITY

Employees of this firm are expected to

_____

_____

_____

_____

_____

_____

_____

_____

_____

_____

_____

Continued on next page

Word Processing Directions

1. Start your word processing software program.

2. Write your employee policy. Proofread and edit your work to make sure that it is correct and concise and provides consequences if not observed.

3. Save your work.

4. Print out a copy of your completed employee policy if your teacher has instructed you to do so.

5. Answer the following questions.

Interpreting Results

1. Why should entrepreneurs provide *written* policies to their employees?

   _____

   _____

   _____

2. Exchange your completed employee policy with a classmate. How does your version differ from your classmate's? Reread your own employee policy. How would you change it after reading your classmate's employee policy?

   _____

   _____

   _____

   _____

   _____

Drawing Conclusions

3. Could small businesses succeed without written policies? Explain.

   _____

   _____

   _____

   _____

   _____

Chapter 14

Chapter 14 Preparing and Planning to Manage

Academic Integration Activity

English Language Arts
Reading Skills

Directions Match each content vocabulary term to its definition. Write the term on the line following the definition.

manager	planning	team building
image	climate	quality control program
controlling	nonverbal communication	operational plans
networking	organizing	time management
human relations	situational management	tactical plans
directing	strategic plans	conceptual skills

1. The process of guiding and supervising employees while they work

   _____

2. The mental picture and feelings people have when thinking of a particular business

   _____

3. The process of allocating time effectively in order to accomplish several objectives

   _____

4. The prevailing atmosphere or attitude of a business

   _____

5. Facial expressions, eye contact, and personal space are examples.

   _____

6. This person coordinates people, processes, and other resources of a business.

   _____

7. The grouping of a business's resources in combinations to accomplish objectives

   _____

8. Using a Web site such as LinkedIn® to make business contacts is an example of this.

   _____

Continued on next page

9. Using logic and reasoning to understand "the big picture" requires this skill set.

_____

10. Activities designed to encourage teamwork and encourage employees to buy into common goals

_____

11. Objectives that help accomplish a business's short-term goals

_____

12. The ability to use whatever management style is appropriate for a particular circumstance

_____

13. Objectives that map out where you want your business to be in three to five years

_____

14. Interpersonal skills key to a manager's ability to lead and manage employees

_____

15. The first step of managing, in which a business's object or desired results are determined

_____

16. A set of measures built into the production process to make sure products or services meet certain standards

_____

17. The final step in managing, in which objectives are measured against actual performance

_____

18. Midrange business objectives meant to be accomplished in one to three years

_____

Chapter 14 Preparing and Planning to Manage
Academic Integration Activity

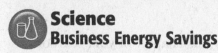

Science
Business Energy Savings

Directions Read the text below, then answer the questions. Show your work on calculations.

ENERGY USE

In terms of total energy consumed, the United States uses more energy than any other country in the world. Most of this energy comes from fossil fuels. The most recent available data shows that 40 percent of the nation's energy comes from petroleum, 24 percent from natural gas, and 23 percent from coal. The rest comes from nuclear power, hydroelectric dams, and various renewable energy sources.

Eleven percent of total energy goes to powering and heating businesses and residences. Many U.S. states and cities have developed programs to reduce overall energy consumption and to encourage more use of renewable energy. One is Energy Trust Oregon, an organization that works with both businesses and homeowners to help find energy solutions and help with the costs of putting these solutions into practice.

For example, Valley Bicycle in Eugene, Oregon, owns a 95-year-old building that once had drafty, cracked windows, very little insulation, and an old, inefficient water heater. An Energy Trust representative visited the business to assess the house and help the owners develop a plan to install replacement windows, blow in wall and crawlspace insulation and replace the water heater. By working with Energy Trust–approved contractors, Valley Bicycle received cash rebates on a percentage of the costs of the work done on the building. Now, a year later, the business's utility bills are lower, the employees feel more comfortable in hot or cold weather, and the building is more energy efficient.

---

1. Valley Bicycle paid an insulation contractor $5,550 for attic and wall insulation. After Energy Trust verified the work was correctly done, they sent the business a rebate check covering 35% of the cost. What did the business end up paying for the insulation?

_____

_____

2. The unit of measure for energy usage is the BTU. Natural gas is measured as BTU per therm, has an energy content of 100,000 BTU per therm, and loses 15% of its energy converting to heat. If Valley Bicycle's natural gas rate is $2.00/therm, what is the cost per million BTU?

_____

_____

Chapter 14 Preparing and Planning to Manage
Case Study Activity
The Netflix Prize

Directions Read the *BusinessWeek* Case Study feature in this chapter of your textbook. Then read the case study below and use the information to answer the questions.

A NETFLIX CONTEST

It was a bold contest that captured the attention of math enthusiasts and computer scientists everywhere. Looking to improve its already popular movie recommendation system, on October 2, 2006, Netflix announced the Netflix Prize. It was a contest offering $1 million to the first individual or team to improve accuracy of movie recommendations by 10 percent or more.

Facing competition from a number of movie-streaming Web sites and from video-rental giant Blockbuster, Netflix decided to let anyone have a crack at improving Cinematch, the recommendation engine that has long given Netflix a leg-up on its rivals. For nearly three years, contestants furiously worked to create a computer algorithm (a list of well-defined instructions for completing a task) that would once and for all know for sure whether a customer would rather watch *Transformers: Rise of the Machines* or *Twilight*. They were aided by Netflix itself, which provided contestants with anonymous user data on movie ratings.

Finally, in the summer of 2009, the BellKor's Pragmatic Chaos team submitted an updated solution that increased accuracy by 10.05%. BellKor's Pragmatic Chaos included two AT&T statisticians, two machine learning researchers, an electrical engineer, a software engineer, and a research scientist. Team member Bob Bell said that no single insight put them over the 10 percent mark. He said that careful studying of data eventually showed patterns that helped lead the team to their breakthrough.

What caused the inaccuracies in the first place? National Public Radio reported that Netflix's inaccuracies were caused by popular yet quirky movies, such as *Napoleon Dynamite*, that got large numbers of ratings indicating people either loved these films or hated them. In a sense, the contest was about how accurately a person's feelings about *Napoleon Dynamite* could be predicted.

---

1. What caused Netflix to decide to improve film recommendations, even though its existing system was already well-liked?

   _____

   _____

   _____

Chapter 14

2. Was Netflix smart to outsource this job to the public instead of hiring professional consultants? Explain why or why not.

_____

_____

_____

_____

_____

_____

_____

_____

_____

_____

3. What function of managing was demonstrated with the Netflix Prize?

_____

_____

_____

_____

_____

_____

_____

_____

_____

_____

_____

_____

_____

Chapter 14 Preparing and Planning to Manage

Test Prep
Sentence Completion

Directions Take the practice test below. Circle the letter of the word or phrase that best completes the following sentence.

1. As a manager, the owner-operator of a business focuses on _____.
   a. growing and expanding the business
   b. creating additional new ventures
   c. coordinating the people, processes, and resources of the operation
   d. selling, stocking, and other operational activities

2. Managerial plans for a period of one year or less are _____.
   a. short-term objectives
   b. operational plans
   c. tactical plans
   d. strategic plans

3. Quality control programs are _____.
   a. programs for organizing people and materials
   b. built-in checks to ensure standards are met
   c. communication directives and assignments to employees
   d. techniques used in planning

4. Using a management approach based on the circumstances is called _____.
   a. power management
   b. routine management
   c. achievement management
   d. situational management

5. Because managers have many things going on at once they need _____.
   a. human-relations skills
   b. problem-solving skills
   c. time-management skills
   d. decision-making skills

6. Managers must be able to see the big picture. Therefore, they need _____.
   a. conceptual skills
   b. broad technical skills
   c. computational skills
   d. two-way communication skills

7. A management style in which a manager tries to maintain control over the whole operation is _____.
   a. an achievement-oriented style
   b. a routine-oriented style
   c. a power-oriented style
   d. a total-quality style

8. Tactical plans are _____.
   a. long-range marketing plans
   b. annual revisions of marketing strategies
   c. short-term adjustments in marketing strategies
   d. midrange objectives built on specific objective dates

9. Effective staff communication is communication that takes place in an atmosphere _____.
   a. of respect and trust
   b. of competition
   c. controlled by a strong manager
   d. of high stress

10. Skills which are a key ingredient in a manager's ability to interact with, lead, and motivate employees are _____.
    a. networking skills
    b. technical skills
    c. human relations skills
    d. time management skills

Chapter 14

Chapter 15 Managing Purchasing and Inventory

 Note Taking

Directions As you read, write notes, facts, and main ideas in the note-taking column. Write key words and short phrases in the cues column. Then summarize the section in the summary box.

Cues	Note Taking
• purchasing	**PURCHASING MANAGEMENT** • Planning purchases involves reviewing sales objectives, then making purchasing decisions, deciding what to buy, from whom to buy, and at what cost.
• financing cost: interest of money borrowed to buy inventory	**INVENTORY MANAGEMENT** • Inventory balance is important. Too little inventory can lead to lost sales; too much inventory leads to increased costs.
Summary	

Chapter 15 Managing Purchasing and Inventory

Section 15.1 Purchasing Management

Section Review: Problem Solving

Directions Ever since you opened your convenience store, you have maintained the same practice when vendors come by with your order. You or your employees would check in vendors by the front door. Once checked in, the vendors move the shipment to the storeroom while you and your employees resume attending to customers. Admittedly, it is a loose way to run an operation. But the system has worked well and kept the time spent on the process at a minimum.

At least it has worked well up until now. Over the last month, several shipments appeared to be short as stock was taken out to price and put on the shelves.

When you spoke to your employees individually, none of them had any idea what happened to the merchandise. In addition, each insists that he or she was thorough when checking in vendors.

You have never had any reason to doubt your employees. Nonetheless, the one-month time frame coincides very closely with the length of employment of your most recent hire. You are very much inclined to fire this employee as the solution to your problem.

Before you make your final decision, take the time to ask yourself the following questions. Your answers might lead to a different decision. Use the Chapter 15 section on receiving and following up purchases and your experience to guide your thinking.

1. What are all the possible causes of the problem?

_____

_____

_____

_____

_____

_____

_____

_____

_____

_____

_____

_____

Continued on next page

2. How could you correct each of the situations (other than the option you considered originally)?

_____

_____

_____

_____

_____

_____

_____

_____

3. What is your best course of action? Identify and explain the one or two most useful strategies for solving the problem. Why did you select these solutions?

_____

_____

_____

_____

_____

_____

_____

_____

_____

_____

_____

_____

_____

_____

Chapter 15

Chapter 15 Managing Purchasing and Inventory

Section 15.2 Inventory Management

Section Review: Planning

Directions Old George is a pretty fair mechanic who owns his own shop down in Ohmigosh, where he is best known for being tight with his money. This story might explain why.

Some years ago George heard there was going to be a shortage of engine blocks due to a union disagreement at a major manufacturer. Since George already did a large amount of business rebuilding engines for the local raceway, he doubled his normal inventory. In order to accomplish this, he got a loan from the local bank. This meant that George now was living on a very tight profit margin. But he figured when the shortage hit, the number of customers would increase substantially, and he would really make a profit then.

Now, he also had problems storing the engines. Since his garage was not very big, he had to put some in a back room. He was a bit concerned about security, but he had never had trouble before.

One month following the purchase and delivery of the engine blocks, the raceway announced that it would be closing. George could not believe his ears. He was ruined!

Years later, George is still fixing engines, but he demands cash up front before he will order a part. Not too long ago, he sold (practically gave) the last of those engines to a neighborhood teenager restoring an old car. Yep, old George is tight with a dollar down in Ohmigosh.

1. What mistakes do you think George made that led to his loss?

_____

_____

_____

_____

_____

_____

_____

_____

_____

_____

_____

Continued on next page

Chapter 15

2. In Chapter 15, the section on inventory management lists six costs associated with too much inventory. Describe those that relate to George's decision and result.

_____

_____

_____

_____

_____

_____

_____

3. What might George have done differently in order to have minimized his risk?

_____

_____

_____

_____

_____

_____

_____

4. What did you learn from George that will be helpful to you as you manage inventory for your business?

_____

_____

_____

_____

_____

_____

_____

_____

_____

_____

Chapter 15

Chapter 15 Managing Purchasing and Inventory

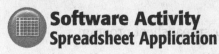
Software Activity
Spreadsheet Application

Directions The objective of this activity is to calculate stock turnover and plan sales.

Business owners can use several calculations to measure the effectiveness of their inventory planning. One of the most often used calculations is the stock turnover rate. Stock turnover measures how many times the store has to replenish its average inventory in a given period and is calculated by dividing sales by average inventory.

The stock turnover rate can also be used to plan sales. Quite frequently, storeowners will determine a stock turnover rate that they wish to achieve. Using past sales records would allow them to estimate the average inventory they will need. Sales can then be calculated by multiplying average inventory by the planned stock turnover rate.

Practice Situation

The printout below shows the amount of average inventories for your store for last year. Calculate the stock turnover rate for the first five departments (Departments 1–5). Calculate sales for the next five departments (Departments 6–10).

Department	Sales	Average Inventory	Stock Turnover Rate
1	$98,456.78	$29,754.12	
2	$1,546,239.00	$100,923.00	
3	$56,832.34	$23,987.00	
4	$29,654.45	$25,982.00	
5	$93,234.21	$39,056.76	
6		$65,234.00	2.5
7		$67,234.75	1.5
8		$87,333.21	2.6
9		$98,234.00	3.1
10		$98,322.11	1.2

Continued on next page

Spreadsheet Directions

1. Start your spreadsheet software program.

2. Re-create the table from the previous page using your spreadsheet program.

3. Enter the formula to calculate stock turnover rate for Departments 1–5. Enter the formula to calculate sales for Departments 6–10.

4. After completing your calculations, save your work.

5. Print out a copy of your work if your teacher has instructed you to do so.

6. Answer the following questions.

Interpreting Results

1. Examine the data for Departments 1–5. Which department has the highest stock turnover rate? Which has the lowest?

_____

_____

2. Examine the data for Departments 6–10. Which department will have the highest planned sales? Which will have the lowest?

_____

_____

Drawing Conclusions

3. After you calculate the stock turnover rate for a department, how do you determine if any improvements are needed?

_____

_____

_____

_____

4. If you plan sales using the stock turnover rate, why might you still not reach your sales goal?

_____

_____

_____

_____

Chapter 15

Chapter 15 Managing Purchasing and Inventory

Academic Integration Activity

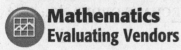
Mathematics
Evaluating Vendors

Directions Mario's Italian Restaurant needs a new pasta vendor. The owner, Mario, is considering four different vendors. Vendor A is 30 miles away and sells pasta for $2.05 a pound. Vendor B is 5 miles away and sells pasta for $2.15 per pound. Vendor C is 50 miles away and sells pasta for $2.07 per pound. Vendor D is 10 miles away and sells pasta for $2.06 per pound.

Each vendor charges $.33 per mile for delivery. The pasta supplied by each vendor is comparable in flavor, quality, and variety.

Mario orders 100 pounds of pasta per week. Vendor A gives a 10 percent discount for any portion of an order over 80 pounds. (On a 100-pound order, 20 pounds would be discounted 10 percent.) Vendor B gives a 5 percent discount for any portion of an order over 50 pounds. Vendor C gives a 10 percent discount for any portion of an order over 100 pounds. Vendor D gives an 8 percent discount for any portion of an order over 75 pounds.

1. Figure the purchase orders below for each vendor.

Mario's Italian Restaurant			
Purchase Order			
VENDOR A			**PURCHASE ORDER NO.: 2001**
QUANTITY	**DESCRIPTION**	**UNIT COST**	**TOTAL**
_____ _____	100 lbs. pasta	$2.05/lb. 1–80 lbs. 10% discount thereafter	_____ _____ Total Amount _____ Shipping _____ Total Due _____

Continued on next page

Chapter 15

Mario's Italian Restaurant
Purchase Order

VENDOR B   **PURCHASE ORDER NO.: 2002**

QUANTITY	DESCRIPTION	UNIT COST	TOTAL
_____	100 lbs. pasta	$2.15/lb. 1–50 lbs. 5% discount thereafter	_____

Total Amount _____

Shipping _____

Total Due _____

Mario's Italian Restaurant
Purchase Order

VENDOR C   **PURCHASE ORDER NO.: 2003**

QUANTITY	DESCRIPTION	UNIT COST	TOTAL
_____	100 lbs. pasta	$2.07/lb. 1–100 lbs. 10% discount thereafter	_____

Total Amount _____

Shipping _____

Total Due _____

Name _____ Date _____ Class _____

Mario's Italian Restaurant

Purchase Order

VENDOR D   PURCHASE ORDER NO.: 2004

QUANTITY	DESCRIPTION	UNIT COST	TOTAL
_____	100 lbs. pasta	$2.06/lb. 1–75 lbs.	_____
_____		8% discount thereafter	
			Total Amount _____
			Shipping _____
			Total Due _____

2. What is the actual price per pound of pasta from each vendor when discounts are calculated and delivery charges are included? (Round to the nearest cent.)

A. _____

_____

B. _____

_____

C. _____

_____

D. _____

_____

3. Based on the prices per pound, which vendor should Mario choose?

_____

_____

_____

_____

_____

_____

_____

_____

Chapter 15 Managing Purchasing and Inventory
Academic Integration Activity
 **Social Studies**
Outlet Stores

Directions Read the text below, follow the steps and answer the questions.

OUTLET STORES

Some manufacturers also have retail stores. These stores do not handle trade or cash discounts, nor do they pay vendors for the goods they sell. *Outlet store* and *factory outlet* are common names for this type of retail operation. The first outlet stores were placed next to company factories, but this setup is rare today. You will often find outlet stores grouped in one location for convenience, a type of shopping center known as an outlet center or outlet mall. In many urban areas outlet centers are placed well outside of the city in a rural area so that the outlet stores do not compete directly with the conventional retailers selling the same products. Despite the distance some shoppers may have to drive to reach outlet centers, these operations are popular because the stores offer deeply discounted prices on popular goods.

---

1. Find the Web site for OutletBound. Look at the home page. What is the function of this Web site?

   _____

   _____

2. On the site, use the correct search engine to find the outlet center nearest to where you live.

   _____

   _____

3. Think of a particular brand you like. Use the correct search engine or the "alpha index" to find the closest outlet store that sells the brand you choose.

   _____

   _____

4. Why do you think outlet stores can offer deeply discounted prices for brand-name goods?

   _____

   _____

   _____

   _____

Chapter 15

Chapter 15 Managing Purchasing and Inventory
Case Study Activity
Warehousing and Distribution

Directions Read the *BusinessWeek* Case Study feature for this chapter in your textbook. Then read the article and use the information to answer the questions.

Giant Warehouses Await Imports That Never Came
By Anton Troianovski

Along a 15-mile stretch of desert in Phoenix, Ariz., nearly a dozen giant warehouses sit silent and empty. They are relics of the city's dream of becoming a national warehouse hub, a vision dashed by plunging imports and a reordering of the nation's biggest ports. Shippers increasingly send goods to ports in Georgia, Virginia, and Florida.

Decisions to site the Phoenix warehouses were made when Americans were buying so many new cars, televisions, and T-shirts that California was running out of cheap storage space. Developers sought to turn the desert on the city's west side into a distribution hub just 370 miles from the Los Angeles ports.

Today, an empty, half-mile-long warehouse lingers from that vision. The building's 1.2 million square feet could fit 193 full-size copies of the Statue of Liberty. Its parking lot has room for 292 tractor trailers. But on a recent morning the only signs of life were a security guard's trailer, golf cart, and bicycle.

Developer Jonathan Tratt's warehouse is one of 13 storage complexes completed in southwest Phoenix in 2008 and 2009. Those 13 properties combined have eight million square feet and are now 86% empty. The construction boom has driven the industrial vacancy rate in the 47 million-square-foot southwest Phoenix market to over 20%. In total, U.S. developers built more industrial real estate during the import boom than office buildings or retail space, as measured by square footage.

Four miles from the security guard's trailer, another 1.2-million square-foot storage building is almost complete and hasn't signed any tenants.

Fortunes in these parts change quickly.

(Excerpted from *The Wall Street Journal*, July 31, 2009)

Continued on next page

Chapter 15

1. In Chapter 9, you learned about site selection and layout planning. What was the reasoning behind the developers' selection of the warehouse sites?

_____

_____

_____

_____

_____

_____

_____

2. What miscalculations did the developers make?

_____

_____

_____

_____

_____

_____

3. Identify the six areas that must be accounted for in warehouse planning.

_____

_____

_____

_____

_____

_____

_____

_____

Chapter 15

Chapter 15 Managing Purchasing and Inventory

Test Prep
Matching

Directions The following statements are comments you might hear from business owners. Match the letter of the inventory costs in the right column with its corresponding statement in the left column. Answer choices may be used more than once.

A. financing costs

B. opportunity costs

C. storage costs

D. insurance costs

E. shrinkage costs

F. obsolescence costs

1. _____ My warehouse roof leaked during the storm and several cases of merchandise were ruined.

2. _____ I have such an overload of stock, I had to rent storage units to put it in.

3. _____ Merchandise has been disappearing overnight.

4. _____ If I could get rid of my dead inventory now, I could get a good deal on a carload of stock.

5. _____ I can't just take my chances that nothing will go wrong.

6. _____ I have a lot of products to sell, but they are out of date.

7. _____ The only thing I can do with these broken materials is just throw them in the garbage.

8. _____ The rent just went up on my warehouse.

9. _____ My cash flow has gotten tighter since interest rates went up and banks got restrictive about lending.

10. _____ The power was out for days and the meat and dairy products went bad.

11. _____ No one wants to buy these cell phones since the updated model with gaming capability came out.

12. _____ As a fireworks retailer, I pay a lot of money to guard against losses and liability in case of an explosion.

13. _____ These billiard tables are popular, but they sure take up a lot of warehouse space.

Continued on next page

Chapter 15

True/False

Directions Circle the **T** if the statement is true and **F** if the statement is false. If the statement is false, write a correct version on the line below.

14. A guiding principle in determining the quantity to purchase is to buy products or materials that match your competitors' inventory.　　**T F**

_____

_____

15. Purchases should be planned to minimize the amount of time that money and storage spaced are tied up.　　**T F**

_____

_____

16. Reliability, distance, and service are factors in choosing a vendor.　　**T F**

_____

_____

17. A key concept in buying products or materials is "the lowest price is the best price."　　**T F**

_____

_____

18. Purchase discounts, if available, should be weighed into final buying decisions.　　**T F**

_____

_____

19. Vendors view late payment for products and materials as an accepted way of doing business.　　**T F**

_____

_____

20. Follow-up on purchases includes keeping track of how well the products or materials work out.　　**T F**

_____

_____

21. A company can have too little inventory, but they can never have too much.　　**T F**

_____

_____

Chapter 16 Production Management and Distribution

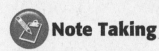**Note Taking**

Directions As you read, write notes, facts, and main ideas in the note-taking column. Write key words and short phrases in the cues column. Then summarize the section in the summary box.

Cues	Note Taking
• product development	**FROM IDEA TO PRODUCT** • Product development is the process of creating or improving products through design, model-building, and testing.
• production management	**PRODUCTION AND DISTRIBUTION** • Manufacturing can be outsourced, but downside is that you have less control over product quality.
	Summary

Chapter 16 Production Management and Distribution

Section 16.1 From Idea to Product

Section Review: Define

Directions One of the best ways to learn about how your business will work is to do a fantasy tour of the business. That is what this activity is designed to do. Take, for example, a simple business that everyone is familiar with and do a fantasy tour. Suppose you are going to start a restaurant where people can come to sit and dine in a casual atmosphere. Now, in your mind, place yourself at the door of the restaurant. You are about to enter for the fantasy tour. Fill out the following table by moving through the restaurant and looking at:

- what task is being performed?
- who is performing the task?
- what equipment do they need to perform the task?

  The first task has been filled in as an example.

Task	Person Performing the Task	Equipment Needed to Do the Task
Greeting the customers and taking reservations	One person	A small desk or podium with an appointment book and menus

Chapter 16 Production Management and Distribution

Section 16.2 Production and Distribution

Section Review: Critical Thinking

Directions In this activity, you will expand on the work you did in the Section 16.1 Activity. This time you are going to create a flowchart of the processes in the business. In any business, many processes happen—making food, serving the customers, taking payment for meals, etc. You need to take the tasks you identified in the previous activity and have the flowchart show how the operations of the business will proceed. As an example, we have taken Task #1 from the previous activity and graphically depicted the process of receiving customers and taking them to their tables. It might look as follows:

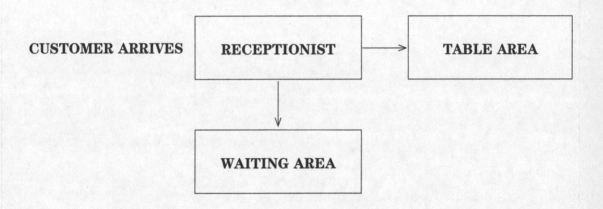

The customer arrives at the receptionist area and is then taken immediately to the table area or is asked to remain in the waiting area until the table is ready.

To create this flowchart, you will need the entire next page. Be sure to connect all tasks in some way because in the business, all operations are interrelated.

Continued on next page

FLOWCHART FOR THE OPERATIONS OF THE RESTAURANT

Chapter 16 Production Management and Distribution

Software Activity
Spreadsheet Application

Directions The objective of this activity is to identify and explain the steps in product development.

Some entrepreneurs must realize that there is usually a long process involved in transforming an idea into a finished, marketable product. This process is known as product development, and it involves a series of steps. These steps usually include: opportunity recognition, concept investigation, product design, and prototype building/testing. Each of these steps is important to the product development process; however, depending upon the idea, entrepreneurs may not approach them in the same sequence.

Practice Situation

You want to develop a new computer game. First, identify activities that entrepreneurs would complete at each step of the product development process. Then, identify the specific steps and tasks you must perform to transform your idea into a marketable product. Make your list clear, concise, and complete. You do not have to use complete sentences; however, the statements need to be easily interpreted by others.

Now you are ready to use this information in developing a slide presentation. Your presentation will identify the steps in the product development process, as well as the specific activities you would have to complete before bringing your idea to the marketplace. Create a series of slides that includes a title slide, and at least one slide for each of the steps in the product development process.

<table>
<tr>
<td>

**Name of
Computer Game**

</td>
<td>

Product Development Process 1
1. Identify Step One
2. Actions to Be Taken
3. Additional Actions to Take

</td>
</tr>
<tr>
<td>

Product Development Process 2
1. Identify Step One
2. Actions to Be Taken
3. Additional Actions to Take

</td>
<td>

Product Development Process 3
1. Identify Step One
2. Actions to Be Taken
3. Additional Actions to Take

</td>
</tr>
</table>

Continued on next page

Spreadsheet Directions

1. Start your PowerPoint software program.

2. Develop a minimum of four slides based on the information you have compiled about the different product development steps needed to transform your idea for a new computer game to a marketable product. You should have at least one slide for each step in the product development process. Some of those slides should include clip art to illustrate the points you are presenting.

3. Save your work.

4. Print out a copy of your slides if your teacher has instructed you to do so.

5. Answer the following questions.

Interpreting Results

1. Which is probably the most important step of the product development process that you have identified?

_____

_____

_____

_____

2. Exchange a copy of your slide presentation with a classmate. Check to determine if the advantages and disadvantages were concisely and clearly written. Identify activities that are not explained clearly. Suggest any additional activities that should be included in order to successfully bring this computer game to the marketplace. Be specific.

_____

_____

_____

_____

Drawing Conclusions

3. If you follow all the steps and activities that you have identified to bring your new computer game to the marketplace, are you guaranteed to be successful? Explain.

_____

_____

_____

_____

_____

Chapter 16 Production Management and Distribution

Academic Integration Activity

English Language Arts
Reading Skills

Directions Circle the letter next to the word or phrase that best completes the sentence.

1. A working model of a product to test with actual customers is called _____.
   a. product development
   b. a prototype
   c. a Gantt chart
   d. quality control

2. Federal Express and United Parcel Service are examples of _____.
   a. contract carriers
   b. logistics
   c. common carriers
   d. private carriers

3. Received shipments are checked for _____.
   a. discrepancies in quantity, price, and discounts
   b. damage
   c. a Gantt chart
   d. delivery terms

4. A market research company being contracted to do customer tests of another company's prototype is an example of _____.
   a. timing the launch
   b. opportunity recognition
   c. outsourcing
   d. concept investigation

5. It is useful to schedule complex projects in the form of _____.
   a. a quality circle
   b. a Gantt chart
   c. a prototype
   d. a PERT diagram

6. Using machines to do the work of people is called _____.
   a. outsourcing
   b. automation
   c. machinery maintenance
   d. logistics

Chapter 16 Production Management and Distribution

Academic Integration Activity

 Social Studies
Planning a Community Service Event

Directions Imagine you are put in charge of a major community service event at your school. It could be anything from tree planting, picking up litter, or painting over graffiti in your community, to participating in Meals on Wheels. These are just some of the possible projects.

Think through the sequence of tasks that you need to organize to make the event run smoothly. Organize the events in a Gantt chart like the diagram below.

Event: _____

Task Number	Task Description			

Key: [ ] **Scheduled Time** [ ] **Progress**

Chapter 16 Production Management and Distribution

Case Study Activity

Increasing Production

Directions Read the *BusinessWeek* Case Study feature in this chapter. Then read the scenario and complete the table.

Assume you are a production assistant for Optimo Fine Hats. As Optimo plans to ramp up its production from 36 to 100 hats per week to stock its new stores, your job is to give a rough estimate of the increased weekly production expenses.

First, calculate the percentage increase from 36 hats to 100 hats: _____

Use the calculated percentage to complete the table.

Expense	Original Cost per Week	Multiplied by	New Cost per Week
Straw (for straw hats)	$775		
Wool felt	1,050		
Peachbloom felt	1,425		
Fur felt	1,540		
Machinery upkeep	275		
Labor	12,300		
Transportation	1,835		
Store rent	2,000		
Storage	230		
Total	**$21,430**		**$59,575.40**

Chapter 16 Production Management and Distribution

Test Prep
Understanding Essay-Test Words

Directions Read the tips for understanding essay test words, then answer the questions.

UNDERSTANDING ESSAY-TEST WORDS
Verbs are key words in essay-test questions and directions. Note the differences between the meanings of these verbs, and keep them in mind when completing an essay test or assignment: • To *evaluate* means to look at the limitations and contributions of an idea.   • To *explain* means to make the meaning of an idea clear.   • To *justify* means to give reasons why an idea was stated.   • To *outline* means to list the main points of an idea.   • To *summarize* means to give a shortened version of an idea.

1. **Explain** why the product development process is considered by some the riskiest part of starting a business.

_____

_____

2. **Outline** the questions small business owners need to consider when deciding whether to handle logistics themselves or outsource it.

_____

_____

3. **Summarize** why using a Gantt chart can help an entrepreneur get through a project.

_____

_____

_____

4. **Justify** a decision by a company that provides bungee jumping to enact a quality control program.

_____

_____

_____

Chapter 17 Managing Operations and Staffing

 Note Taking

Directions As you read, write notes, facts, and main ideas in the note-taking column. Write key words and short phrases in the cues column. Then summarize the section in the summary box.

Cues	Note Taking
• policy	**MANAGING OPERATIONS** • Operational plans govern day-to-day business operations and may be delegated to employees as the business grows.
• line organization	**STAFFING AND COMPANY POLICIES** • Organizational charts set up organization structure, showing how jobs are related and helping delegate responsibility.
Summary	

Chapter 17 Managing Operations and Staffing
Section 17.1 Managing Operations
Section Review: Identify

Directions In Chapter 17, the three Cs of credit were identified as *character*, *capacity*, and *capital*. Each of the following statements addresses one of these. Identify which by writing the correct term in the space provided to the left of each sentence.

1. _____ The applicant owns three homes.

2. _____ The applicant filed for bankruptcy one month ago.

3. _____ The applicant has a large savings account.

4. _____ A credit check on the applicant reveals several delinquent accounts.

5. _____ The applicant has been unemployed for six months.

6. _____ A business contacts the credit bureau regarding all new applications for credit.

7. _____ The applicant's monthly bills equal 50 percent of his/her monthly income.

8. _____ The applicant has a large stock portfolio.

9. _____ The applicant has no previous credit history.

10. _____ The applicant collects classic cars.

11. _____ The applicant has a half-dozen credit cards and charge accounts and keeps payments current on all of them.

12. _____ The applicant is making monthly payments on a number of large loans—education, new car, condominium mortgage, and personal.

13. _____ The applicant has reached the credit limits on all of his or her bank cards and charge accounts.

14. _____ The applicant's assets are limited to an older model car and a small checking account.

15. _____ The applicant has a credit history that goes back more than 15 years.

16. _____ The applicant works two jobs.

Chapter 17 Managing Operations and Staffing

Section 17.2 Staffing and Company Policies

Section Review: Apply

Directions The object of this game is to pin the right position on the blocks of a business's organization chart.

In the box below is a list of positions you have to work with. Unless otherwise indicated (by a number in parentheses), there is only one of each. Check them off as you place them in the chart on page 214. *Hint:* It will help if you first decide which jobs are line positions and which are staff. This will narrow the number of potential placements for some of them.

Chapter 17

```
            Accountant

        Advertising Specialist

    Customer Service Representative

              Manager

           Office Manager

              Owner

          Purchasing Agent

            Receptionist

            Sales Manager

      Sales Representatives (3)

          Secretaries (3)

           Shipping Clerk

         Warehouse Manager
```

1. Distribute the named personnel in the organization chart on the next page. As you work, remember organization chart conventions (like the significance of solid and broken lines).

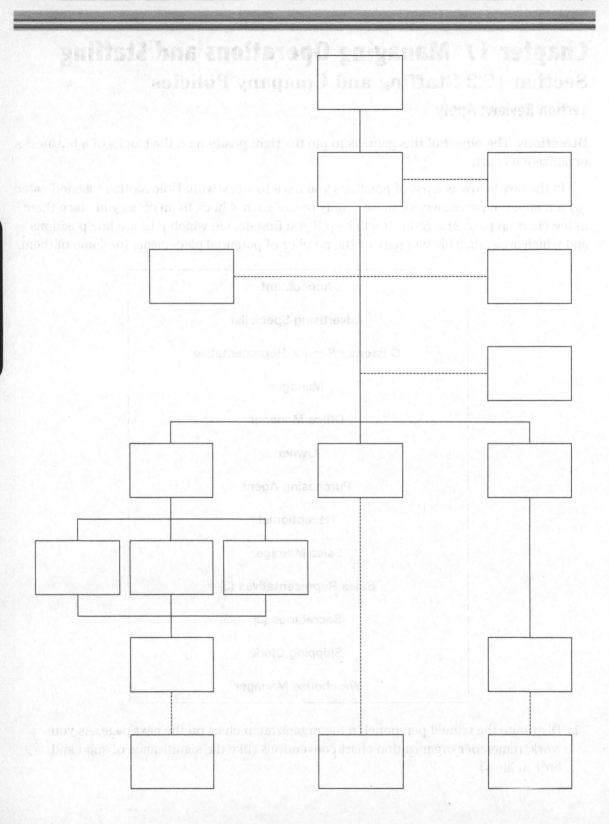

2. Explain how you decided which positions were line personnel and which were staff. Refer to the chapter definitions of these terms to justify your answers.

_____

_____

_____

_____

_____

_____

_____

3. How would this chart be helpful to a manager working in the business?

_____

_____

_____

_____

_____

_____

_____

_____

4. How would this chart be useful to other employees of the business?

_____

_____

_____

_____

_____

_____

_____

_____

_____

Chapter 17 Managing Operations and Staffing

Software Activity
Spreadsheet Application

Directions The objective of this activity is to write a job description.

Practice Situation

You are opening a new business that will require you to hire an office/credit manager. The employment agency that you are using has asked you to develop a job description for this position. Below is a list of tasks the office/credit manager would need to perform:

- prepare bank deposits
- list checks and cash with each bank deposit
- check sales tickets for accuracy
- check sales tickets for completeness of the information provided
- take deposits to the bank daily
- keep sales and expense record sheets
- post sales and expenses
- process credit applications
- send out collection notices to past due accounts

- check invoices of outside purchases to verify receipt, quantity received, and price
- obtain store manager's approval for all invoices
- maintain inventories
- complete all accounting and prepare periodic financial statements
- assist on sales floor and in other areas when needed

Write a concise job description based on the information above. Job tasks should be presented in a logical sequence. A suggested heading has been included to get you started (see below). If you wish to alter the heading, simply replace the one provided with your own.

JOB DESCRIPTION

Job Title: Office/Credit Manager
Supervisor: Store Manager

_____

_____

_____

_____

_____

_____

_____

_____

Word Processing Directions

1. Start your word processing software program.

2. Write the job description. Proofread and edit your work to make sure that it is correct and concise.

3. Save your work.

4. Print out a copy of your completed job description if your teacher has instructed you to do so.

5. Answer the following questions.

Interpreting Results

1. What other uses might entrepreneurs have for job descriptions after the hiring process?

_____

_____

_____

_____

_____

2. Exchange your completed job description with a classmate. How does your version differ from your classmate's? Reread your own job description. How would you change it after reading your classmate's job description?

_____

_____

_____

_____

Drawing Conclusions

3. Why is it important to have a job description for each position in a firm?

_____

_____

_____

_____

_____

Chapter 17 Managing Operations and Staffing
Academic Integration Activity

Mathematics
Piece Rate

Directions Some jobs pay on a piece rate basis. Employees are paid a certain amount for each item of work they produce.

Use the following formula for calculating the answers to the following questions:

Total Pay = Rate per Item × Number Produced

1. Christian Olfert works for Drummond Machine Company. He earns $1.30 for every molding he presses. What is his total pay for a week in which he presses 340 moldings?

_____

2. Kelly Cantor delivers newspapers for *The Melodyville Standard*. He is paid $0.08 for every daily paper (Mon.–Fri.) he delivers and $0.75 for every Sunday paper. What is his pay for a week in which he delivers 454 daily papers and 132 Sunday papers?

_____

3. During the spring Nina Milling assembles bicycles at The Wheeler Dealer. She is paid $13.50 for each bicycle assembled during a regular work week, $14.50 for each bicycle assembled on a Saturday, and $16.00 for each bicycle assembled on a Sunday. What is her total pay for a week in which she assembled the following number of bicycles?

Mon.	Tues.	Wed.	Thurs.	Fri.	Sat.	Sun.
4	7	6	10	8	4	5

4. James Hosford has a job with the Acme Bottling Company. He fills cartons with bottles, seals the cartons, and stacks them on pallets. Monday through Friday he is paid $0.51 for each carton he fills. On Saturday he is paid an additional $0.23 for each carton he fills. What is his total pay for a week in which he filled the following number of cartons?

Mon.	Tues.	Wed.	Thurs.	Fri.	Sat.
210	175	224	160	216	90

5. Amy Chang works in the upholstery department of a furniture factory. She upholsters couches, loveseats, and chairs. She receives $100 for each couch, $80 for each loveseat, and $70 for each chair. During the last 4 weeks she upholstered 6 couches, 5 loveseats, and 5 chairs.

   a. What is her total pay for the 4 weeks?

   b. If she worked 120 hours, what was her hourly rate?

_____

Chapter 17 Managing Operations and Staffing

Academic Integration Activity

Social Studies
Conducting Job Interviews

Directions For this activity, divide into pairs for a role-playing exercise. Using the interview guidelines on page 406 of your book as a guide, come up with possible questions and answers for an imaginary job interview. (The job does not to have to be anything specific.) Take turns as interviewer and interviewee. One question and answer has been provided to help get you started.

1. Question: What are your strengths? _____

   Answer: I have skills that transfer well from one industry to another, such as good communication
   skills, strong math skills, and versatility with computers and software. _____

2. Question: _____

   Answer: _____
   _____

3. Question: _____

   Answer: _____
   _____

4. Question: _____

   Answer: _____
   _____

5. Question: _____

   Answer: _____
   _____

6. Question: _____

   Answer: _____
   _____

7. Question: _____

   Answer: _____
   _____

8. Question: _____

   Answer: _____
   _____

9. Question: _____

Answer: _____

_____

10. Question: _____

Answer: _____

_____

11. Question: _____

Answer: _____

_____

12. Question: _____

Answer: _____

_____

13. Question: _____

Answer: _____

_____

14. Question: _____

Answer: _____

_____

15. Question: _____

Answer: _____

_____

Add any other questions and answers you can think of.

_____

_____

_____

_____

_____

_____

_____

_____

Chapter 17 Managing Operations and Staffing
Case Study Activity
Supermarket Strategies

Directions Read the *BusinessWeek* Case Study feature in this chapter. Then read the article and answer the questions that follow.

SUPERMARKET STRATEGIES: WHAT'S NEW AT THE GROCER
By Damian Joseph

Today's newly frugal consumers are cranking up the pressure on retailers to innovate. Though an average grocery store has 46,852 items, the sector's big chains also stock pretty much the same brand-name goods. So with little room to further cut prices or wow consumers with unique products, food retailers are seeking out new trends and technology that might differentiate them from competitors. "Grocery stores lose or gain about 10 percent of their customer base each year," says Neil Stern, a senior partner at Chicago-based retail consultancy McMillan Doolittle. "So the question is: Can you grab your share of new customers?"

One way a grocer can impress consumers is to get out of the way. Smart shopping carts, mobile coupons, and self-checkout lanes let consumers help themselves. They can pull up product reviews; keep a running tab by scanning goods as they are placed in a cart; download coupons for them on cell phones; and pay without ever entering a line.

Another tool is convenience. With most people on tight schedules, fewer shoppers want to go out of their way for food. Large chains are filling in the gaps between their bigger locations with smaller stores and stocking them with ready-made meals, basics, and extras like in-store baby-sitters. The average sale might be smaller, but the repeat business can add up.

As the purchasing power of minorities grows, grocers are increasingly attempting to accommodate their tastes. Wal-Mart's Supermercado and Publix's Sabor are examples of smaller, ethnic stores that cater to Latinos or immigrants from Asia and the Middle East. More employees are bilingual, too.

And now, there's no place for a customer to escape targeted advertising. Wal-Mart spent two years and $10 million developing Smart Network, an advanced in-store television market that can provide detailed product info and control the ads on each individual screen. The conveyor belts at Kroger's cashier stations are being branded, too.

Meantime, Walgreens and Wal-Mart are testing embedded microchips that let employees know when to restock empty shelves and track in-store advertising. A Procter & Gamble trial boosted sales nearly 20%.

Supermarkets may not be able to pull shoppers away from the competition by putting soda on sale, but convenience, green products, or a ready-to-eat meal just might do the trick.

Excerpted from *BusinessWeek*, June 9, 2009

Continued on next page

1. According to the article, what percentage of their customer base do grocery stores gain or lose each year?

_____

2. List the five tools that grocers are using to impress customers.

_____

_____

_____

_____

_____

_____

3. Outline a situation in which you might go to a chain's bigger location. Then outline a situation in which you would prefer one of the smaller stores described in the article.

_____

_____

_____

_____

_____

4. Explain how the targeted advertising efforts might backfire on the stores that employ them.

_____

_____

_____

_____

_____

5. Recall the Case Study feature from the book. Why might Publix's employees be motivated to make sure that the new trends and innovations are smoothly implemented?

_____

_____

_____

_____

_____

Chapter 17 Managing Operations and Staffing

Test Prep
Unmatching

Directions Circle the term that does not belong. Then explain your choice on the lines below.

1. handling complaints   no smoking   order response time   hours of operation

_____

_____

_____

_____

2. "Employees shall wear name tags at all times."

   "All food and beverages must remain behind the counter."

   "All employees receive two weeks paid vacation each year."

   "Paychecks will be distributed after 1 P.M. only."

_____

_____

_____

_____

3. owner/manager   attorney   salesperson   delivery person

_____

_____

_____

4 payroll clerk   training director   buyer   network administrator

_____

_____

_____

_____

Continued on next page

Chapter 17

5. line-and-staff organization task-team task team organization
project organization

_____

_____

_____

_____

6. nature of job job pay job duties job responsibilities

_____

_____

_____

_____

7. résumés skills and abilities experiences responsibilities

_____

_____

_____

_____

8. classified ads employment agencies applications word-of-mouth

_____

_____

_____

_____

9. piece rate commission bonus hourly rate

_____

_____

_____

_____

10. family history records payroll records I-9 forms medical records

_____

_____

_____

_____

Chapter 17

Chapter 18 Managing Human Resources

 Note Taking

Directions As you read, write notes, facts, and main ideas in the note-taking column. Write key words and short phrases in the cues column. Then summarize the section in the summary box.

Cues	Note Taking
• human resources, h.r. management	**DEVELOPING AND KEEPING HUMAN RESOURCES** • Human resources = personnel. They offer labor, character, ethics, creativity, intellectual energy, social and business connections.
• Theory X	**MOTIVATING EMPLOYEES** • Communication is key to motivating employees. Regard for and treatment of employees is also important.
Summary	

Chapter 18

Chapter 18 Managing Human Resources

Section 18.1 Developing and Keeping Human Resources

Section Review: Compare and Contrast

Directions You are the owner of a small computer business, and one of your employees has just resigned. She filled an important management position in your company.

Several employees in the company might be able to fill the position. But you also know of three people who are currently working for competitors who might be interested in the position.

You must decide whether to recruit internally or externally. You should take into consideration the positive and negative consequences of the decision you make.

1. What are the advantages of selecting someone from within the organization to fill the position? What are the disadvantages?

_____

_____

_____

_____

_____

_____

_____

_____

_____

_____

_____

_____

_____

_____

_____

_____

_____

_____

_____

Chapter 18

2. What are the advantages of selecting an employee from a competitor? What are the disadvantages?

_____

_____

_____

_____

_____

_____

_____

_____

_____

_____

3. How would you decide?

_____

_____

_____

_____

_____

_____

_____

_____

_____

_____

_____

_____

_____

_____

Chapter 18

Chapter 18 Managing Human Resources

Section 18.2 Motivating Employees

Section Review: Apply

Directions Read the scenario, then answer the questions.

John had worked for a small public relations firm for 15 years. He had held the same graphic design position for most of the time he had been employed there.

John was a good employee. He was rarely absent, came to work on time, did his job with little comment, and went home.

Recently, the firm began to update equipment and alter the production process. New, more complex design software replaced the software the company had been using for several years. Many employees, including John, had to learn new skills. John's incidents of absenteeism increased, and his overall job performance was noticeably lower than before. It seemed John was no longer as motivated as before.

1. What would you do to remotivate John?

   _____

   _____

   _____

   _____

   _____

2. How would you keep him motivated?

   _____

   _____

   _____

   _____

   _____

3. Can you think of anything that could have been done to prevent the change in John?

   _____

   _____

   _____

   _____

   _____

Chapter 18 Managing Human Resources

 ## Software Activity
PowerPoint Application

Directions The objective of this activity is to identify steps required to orient and train a new employee.

Once entrepreneurs begin hiring employees to work in their firm, they must orient and train them in their new jobs. Depending upon the size and complexity of the firm, this training will take various forms. Some entrepreneurs who own very small businesses may rely solely on informal, on-the-job training. Many entrepreneurs provide formal orientation/training to new employees in the form of workshops/seminars or written training manuals.

Practice Situation

Select a job task that would be performed by one employee at a business you are familiar with. Identify all the steps needed to complete the task. Then, identify standards against which the employee's performance on this task will be evaluated. Make your list clear and concise. You do not have to use complete sentences; however, the statements need to be easily interpreted by others.

Use this information to develop a slide presentation that will identify the steps required of an employee successfully completing the job task. Develop a series of slides (like the ones presented below) that could be used in providing training to a new employee in a formal setting.

Receptionist

Responsibilities:
- Answer phones
- Take messages
- Log in deliveries

Receptionist

Requirements:
- Knowledge of phone system
- Verbal/written skills
- High school diploma

Continued on next page

Spreadsheet Direction

1. Start your PowerPoint software program.

2. Based on the information you have developed for training a new employee on a specific job task, develop a series of slides. Include clip art on some of these slides.

3. Save your work.

4. Print out a copy of your completed job description if your teacher has instructed you to do so.

5. Answer the following questions.

Interpreting Results

1. What problems could result from informal, on-the-job training?

_____

_____

_____

_____

2. Use your slides to train a classmate in the job task you have identified. Consider the classmate's feedback. Were there statements that were unclear? Did you omit any steps that would be crucial to training employees? Revise your slides based on this input.

_____

_____

_____

_____

_____

_____

Drawing Conclusions

3. After entrepreneurs implement a training program, what must occur next?

_____

_____

_____

_____

_____

Chapter 18 Managing Human Resources
Academic Integration Activity

 English Language Arts
Reading Skills

Directions Match each content vocabulary term to its definition by writing the letter of the term on the line provided.

a. Theory X
b. hygiene factors
c. Pregnancy Discrimination Act
d. educational activities
e. cost effective
f. employee complaint procedure
g. Theory Y
h. telecommuting

i. flextime
j. human resources
k. performance evaluation
l. labor union
m. developmental activities
n. motivating factors
o. family leave

_____ 1. The people employed in a business

_____ 2. Workers join these organizations to strengthen their bargaining ability.

_____ 3. Economically worthwhile in terms of the money spent to get the result

_____ 4. The belief that employees like to work

_____ 5. Actions that prepare employees for advancement in an organization

_____ 6. Formal procedure for dealing with employee concerns

_____ 7. Short-run solutions that keep situations from getting worse

_____ 8. One of the laws and regulations designed to protect employees

_____ 9. Achievement, recognition, and responsibility are among them.

_____ 10. Some or all of the job is performed away from the business.

_____ 11. Process of judging how well an employee has performed his or her job

_____ 12. A work schedule that takes into account the employee's personal life

_____ 13. The belief that employees are lazy and need supervision

_____ 14. Time off work for an event such as a birth, death, or family illness

_____ 15. Actions designed to prepare managers to prepare for the future

Chapter 18

Chapter 18 Managing Human Resources
Academic Integration Activity

Social Studies
The Influence of Managers

Directions In the section "How Managers Influence Motivation," Douglas McGregor's Theory X and Theory Y were discussed. You are now going to do your own research to discover how people around you think.

Using the questionnaire below, interview five people and record their responses. Mark 5 if they strongly agree, 1 if they strongly disagree, or some number in between. Try to be as accurate as possible. After you collect all the data from the questionnaires, assess the interviewees' potential as future managers based on the questions that follow the questionnaire.

		Strongly Agree				Strongly Disagree
1.	People do not like work and try to avoid it.	5	4	3	2	1
2.	Managers have to push people, closely supervise them, or threaten them with punishment to get them to produce.	5	4	3	2	1
3.	People have little or no ambition and will try to avoid responsibility.	5	4	3	2	1
4.	Work is natural to people and is actually an important part of their lives.	5	4	3	2	1
5.	People will work toward goals if they are committed to them.	5	4	3	2	1
6.	People become committed to goals when it is clear that achieving them will bring personal rewards.	5	4	3	2	1
7.	Under the right conditions, people not only accept responsibility but also seek it out.	5	4	3	2	1
8.	People have a high degree of imagination, ingenuity, and creativity, all of which can be used in solving an organization's problems.	5	4	3	2	1
9.	Employees have much more potential than organizations actually use.	5	4	3	2	1

Chapter 18 *(side tab)*

1. Using your own judgment, how many of the five people interview___
managers? What makes you think so? Do they tend to make Theory ___
assumptions?

_____

_____

_____

_____

2. Based on what you think makes a good manager, what would be the highest score an
interviewee could attain? What would be the lowest? Show how you calculate this.

_____

_____

_____

_____

_____

3. What did you learn about your interviewees' attitude concerning motivation?

_____

_____

_____

_____

_____

4. Has your attitude about motivation changed after carrying out this questionnaire and
reading the chapter? Do you agree or disagree with the authors that those who hold
Theory Y assumptions make the best managers?

_____

_____

_____

_____

_____

Chapter 18

Human Resources

...se Study feature in this chapter. Then read the arti-
...w.

LESSON OF *CORALINE*
By Jessie Scanlon

...ntasy movie directed by Henry Selick, brought in almost
...ce receipts in its first week. This week I saw the innovative tech-
...d the movie: Objet Geometries' Connex500.

The Connex500 is a 3-D printer. It can take an object designed in any animation program and "print" a physical copy. Very simply, the software slices the design into microns-thick layers, and gives the printer a footprint for each, so that it can build a model one layer at a time. Because the Connex has multiple printer heads, it can build an object out of any of Objet's eight basic plastic materials—which range from rigid to flexible, and include clear, white, and black options—or combine them to create an infinite number of blends.

Coraline is a stop-motion animation film, an incredibly time-consuming and model-driven process. (It's like a cartoon strip except that every frame is a photograph of a physical set or model rather than a drawing.) When Selick directed *Nightmare Before Christmas*, also a stop-motion film, he used hand-made models to give the main character 800 potential expressions. Thanks to 3-D printing, Selick was able to give Coraline 208,000 potential expressions by using 320 interchangeable molds of different eyebrow and forehead expressions and 650 different mouth molds.

Entertainment is a growing but relatively new sector for Objet, according to president Frank Marangell, who describes its clients as Fortune 500 companies in consumer products, medical devices, footwear, toys, consumer electronics, automotive, and other industries.

Excerpted from *BusinessWeek*, February 22, 2009

---

1. Use an Internet search engine to find the company Web site for Objet Geometries. Find the "Company" drop-down tab. Research the company and write a paragraph describing Objet, including a company overview, its vision statement, and information about its worldwide offices. Use another sheet of paper to write your paragraph.

_____

_____

2. Describe a scenario in which Pixar and Objet might do business.

_____

_____

Name _____ Date _____ Class _____

Chapter 18 Managing Human Resources

Test Prep
Memory Helpers

Directions Read the tips for helping your memory, then draw a quick visual reminder for each of the statements below.

MEMORY HELPERS
• Write down what you want to remember.   • Keep all your notes for each class together so you can find them easily.   • Believe in yourself. If you keep saying you have a bad memory, you will.   • Create visual images of the things you want to remember. You can create quick, simple drawings in your notes next to words.

1. Human resources are the people employed in a business.

2. An employment complaint procedure should be put in writing and distributed to employees.

3. Telecommuting involves performing some or all of the job away from the business.

4. Flextime allows employees to choose the work hours and days that are most effective for their personal lives.

Chapter 19 Financing Your Business

 ## Note Taking

Directions As you read, write notes, facts, and main ideas in the note-taking column. Write key words and short phrases in the cues column. Then summarize the section in the summary box.

Cues	Note Taking
• bootstrapping	**FINANCING THE SMALL BUSINESS START-UP** • Short-term entrepreneurial needs include such things as cost of start-up, or purchasing more inventory than normal. Long-term needs relate to future growth, such as buying capital assets.
• pro forma	**OBTAINING FINANCING AND GROWTH CAPITAL** • Pro forma: Proposed or estimated financial statements based on predictions on how business operations will turn out. These are included in financial requests.
Summary	

Chapter 19 Financing Your Business

Section 19.1 Financing the Small Business Start-Up

Section Review: Examine

Directions As you look into ways to finance your start-up business, there will be many different potential sources you might consider. One way to think about these options is by comparing available statistics. Here is an exercise to get you started.

The federal government helps small businesses through the Small Business Administration because these companies are so important to the national economy. Venture capitalists, on the other hand, invest in companies in return for such things as a percentage of the profits or partial control of the company's affairs. Study the table and determine the average size of an SBA loan and a venture capital investment. Then answer the following questions.

	Year 1	Year 2	Year 3
SBA loans granted	19,300	18,800	38,800
Value of total loans	$3,217,000,000	$4,354,000,000	$8,426,000,000
Value of average loan	_____	_____	_____
Venture capital investment granted	NA	NA	972*
Value of total investment	NA	NA	$3,098,395,000
Value of average investment			_____

*Some companies received more than one investment at different stages of a project.

1. Compare the size of an average SBA loan and an average venture capital investment in Year 3.

_____

_____

2. Compare the number of loans with the number of investments.

_____

3. Why do you think these differences occur?

_____

_____

_____

_____

_____

Chapter 19

Section 19.2 Obtaining Financing and Growth Capital

Section Review: Show

Directions For the last 10 chapters, you have been collecting information for your business plan. Now you must take all of the information you have gathered and make some sense of it. The Business Proposal Assessment that appears on the next several pages can help.

Take a look at the plan to see how it is organized. Fill out as much information as you can and think about how you want to present your business to potential investors, partners, and employees. Remember, this is only a draft. However, you may want to schedule an appointment with a professional for advice and tips on how to improve your plan.

The Ohio Small Business Development Center
Business Proposal Assessment   **BUSINESS PLAN GUIDE**

Please complete this questionnaire and have it available when you meet with the SBDC counselor. Attach additional sheets as needed.

Name:_____

Company Name (if known):_____

Address:_____

Phone:_____

1. Describe the product/service you are planing to offer in your business. Be sure to include specifically what the product/service will do for your customers, the methods or technologies to be used, the business location, and the geographic area to be served.
   (**For a Product:** Specify if manufacturing or other, business or consumer market, etc.)
   (**For a Service:** Specify the type of service, i.e., retailing, a business or a consumer service, etc.)
   Describe product/service:_____

   _____

   _____

   _____

   _____

2. Is this business...
   [ ] A new business   [ ] An expansion of a current business   [ ] A takeover of an existing business
   [ ] Other type of business (Describe) _____
   [ ] Not sure what business will be

Chapter 19

3. Is your business going to be a...
   [ ] Sole Proprietorship   [ ] Corporation
   [ ] Partnership—Who will your partners be?_____
   [ ] Other type of business (Describe)_____
   [ ] Not sure what type business will be

4. Why are you going into this business? Think about your financial and non-financial goals.
   Financial goals: _____
   _____
   _____

   Non-financial goals:_____
   _____
   _____

I. Marketing Issues

5. Who is your target market (i.e., potential customers)? For consumer products/services, be sure to include general demographic information (such as age, income, gender, etc.) and behavior characteristics (such as lifestyles, opinion, etc). For business products/services, include the business classifications or descriptions and the size of the business you will serve.
   _____
   _____
   _____
   _____

6. Describe your target market's buying habits. Think about information such as seasonal/cyclical demand patterns, frequency of purchase, competitive contracts, customized contracts, or price lists, etc.
   _____
   _____
   _____

7. Describe your primary competitors (include name and locations, sales patterns, etc.) and explain a little bit about how well their businesses are doing. Also explain a little about the industry and any relevant changes within the industry.
   _____
   _____
   _____

Continued on next page

Chapter 19

8. Why do you think customers will buy from you? (Include product/service benefits, strengths, weaknesses, as well as potential and marketable differences between your product/service and competitors' products/services).

_____

_____

_____

9. Describe the size of the current market and about what percent of the market you think you may get. Think about the market's historic (last 3–5 years) and future (next 2–3 years) growth rate.

_____

_____

_____

10. Describe your future new markets (such as geographic locations, new customers, etc.) or new products (additions to the line or new lines).

_____

_____

_____

11. Describe how the product/service will reach the target market. Think about sales and distribution methods.

_____

_____

_____

12. Please list the factors you have considered in your location decision (such as costs/overhead, zoning laws, building codes and standards, options for expansion, traffic flow, etc.).

_____

_____

_____

13. How do you plan to communicate or advertise your product offerings to your target market?

_____

_____

_____

Chapter 19

14. How is your product/service priced compared to the competition?

[ ] Higher

[ ] Same

[ ] Lower

[ ] Don't know

15. Explain how you decided to price your product. Include a completed cost and profit margins analysis (attach if necessary).

_____

_____

_____

II. Management Issues

16. Describe your educational background and managerial experience in this type of business. Include all types of related or transferable experience.

_____

_____

17. To which related trade or business organizations do you belong?

_____

_____

18. What managerial, staff, and operational positions have you identified, and what duties will they have? What skills do they need?

Position	Duties	Skills
_____	_____	_____
_____	_____	_____

19. Which records have you thought about using to control your business?

[ ] Payroll

[ ] Sales/Accounts Receivable

[ ] Inventory

[ ] Purchases/Accounts Payable

[ ] Other (Describe)_____

Continued on next page

Chapter 19

III. Equipment and Inventory

20. What equipment and inventory items are required to start and run this business? Attach a complete list if available.

_____

_____

_____

21. Describe what you know about the potential suppliers of the items you need for your business.

_____

_____

_____

IV. Taxes, Insurance, and Regulations

22. What taxes apply to your business? Who will prepare your taxes?

_____

_____

_____

23. What have you learned from an insurance agent about the type of insurance you will need and how much it will cost?

_____

_____

_____

24. Which local, state, and federal regulations and licenses have you determined apply to your business?

_____

_____

_____

V. Financial

25. Attach a copy of your business's cash flow projections. Explain below which issues you have considered in your cash-flow statement, such as the length of time customers take to pay, the total cost of labor, the cost of delivery, the cost of mailings, etc.

_____

_____

_____

26. Attach pro-forma income statement.

27. Attach break-even analysis.

28. Attach pro-forma balance sheet.

29. Attach a personal financial statement.

30. What is the minimum amount you need per month to take home from the business to live on? $ _____ /Month

31. How much money are you willing to retain in the business to help it grow? $ _____

32. Explain how you will handle cash flow problems if sales don't cover expenses or accounts receivable are late?

_____

_____

33. How much will you need in total to start your business? $ _____

34. About what percent of this money will come from...
    Personal funds   _____ %
    Borrow from family   _____ %
    Borrow from bank   _____ %
    Seek private investors _____ %
           TOTAL   100%

35. Explain specifically what this money will be used for?

_____

_____

36. What assets are you willing to use as collateral against money you are borrowing? Be sure to speak with anyone who may also be affected by you using this as collateral.
    [ ] Nothing   [ ] House or personal real estate   [ ] Car
    [ ] Other (Specify) _____

37. Are you willing to give up ownership rights in the company or share ownership?
    [ ] Yes   [ ] No
    [ ] Would definitely prefer not to, but would if required

38. Who will be responsible for your debts (i.e., co-signer) if the business fails? Be sure you have consulted with this person.

_____

_____

_____

Chapter 19

Chapter 19 Financing Your Business

 **Software Activity**
Spreadsheet Application

Directions The objective of this activity is to calculate start-up costs.

Startup costs are the expenses that entrepreneurs will have when they are first setting up their businesses. To identify start-up costs, entrepreneurs must review every aspect of their business plan, and list everything they will have to spend money on before the business even opens.

Practice Situation

You have listed and estimated the start-up expenses for your new business on the printout shown below. Use your spreadsheet program to calculate a subtotal for each category and a total for all expenses.

START-UP COSTS		
	Total Funds Required	**Subtotals/Totals**
FIXED ASSETS		
Equipment	$12,060	
Fixtures and Furniture	$30,850	
(Subtotal)		
PRE-PAID ITEMS AND DEPOSITS		
Rent, Deposits, and Insurance	$1,650	
Taxes, Licenses, and Fees	$150	
(Subtotal)		
PRE-OPENING EXPENSES		
Training, Advertising, and Promotion	$2,300	
Legal and Accounting Services	$2,000	
(Subtotal)		
INVENTORY AND SUPPLIES		
Goods Purchased	$80,000	
Supplies	$2,600	
(Subtotal)		
WORKING CAPITAL		
Petty Cash	$200	
Projected Cash Deficits	$5,000	
Three Months' Operating Expenses	$28,500	
(Subtotal)		
TOTALS		

Chapter 19

Spreadsheet Directions

1. Start your spreadsheet software program.

2. Re-create the table from the previous page using your spreadsheet program.

3. In column 3, enter the formula to calculate the subtotal for each of the categories listed. After calculating each subtotal, enter the formula for a total of all start-up expenses.

4. After completing your calculations, save your work.

5. Print out a copy of your work if your teacher has instructed you to do so.

6. Answer the following questions.

Interpreting Results

1. Examine the data for each of the subtotals. Which category has the highest expenses? Which has the lowest?

   _____

   _____

2. What are the total start-up expenses required for this business?

   _____

   _____

Drawing Conclusions

3. Many of these expenses are based on estimate. What will be the impact of underestimating specific expenses?

   _____

   _____

   _____

   _____

   _____

4. Will an entrepreneur be able to borrow funds to cover all these start-up expenses?

   _____

   _____

   _____

   _____

   _____

Chapter 19

Chapter 19 Financing Your Business

Academic Integration Activity

English Language Arts
Writing Skills

Directions Pick nine of the 12 content vocabulary terms and use each in a sentence that shows you understand the meaning of the term as it is used in the chapter.

bootstrapping	angel	initial public offering
factor	pro forma	stock
equity	capacity	working capital
line of credit	due diligence	contingency fund

1. _____

_____

2. _____

_____

3. _____

_____

4. _____

_____

5. _____

_____

6. _____

_____

7. _____

_____

8. _____

_____

9. _____

_____

Chapter 19

Chapter 19 Financing Your Business
Academic Integration Activity

 **Social Studies**
Business Financing

Directions Read the article, then answer the questions.

Small Businesses: Excitement and Risk

By definition, a small business in the United States generally employs 100 or fewer people. This business can take several forms: a corporation, a partnership, or a sole proprietorship. Starting a business is an exciting adventure for the entrepreneur, but it is also full of risks. The entrepreneur invests a considerable amount of money, time, and talent into his or her new company, but dreams of independence and wealth can quickly be dashed. According to the U.S. Small Business Administration (SBA), an independent agency of the federal government, approximately 33 percent of new businesses fail within two years; 56 percent fail within four years.

What can small business owners do to survive and then thrive? One key is to have enough capital, money used to start a business, to get through the challenging early months or years of the company's life. Another is to avoid or limit obtaining capital through the use of credit cards, which have much higher interest rates than interest paid on a line of credit or bank loan.

1. Find the Web site for the U.S. Small Business Administration. From the home page, click on "About SBA." What is the function of the SBA?

   _____

   _____

2. From the home page, click on the "Small Business Planner" tab. List the steps for each stage of business development listed in the planner.

   _____

   _____

3. From the home page, find the "Services" tab. List the services SBA offers under the "Financial Assistance" heading.

   _____

   _____

   _____

4. Write a few sentences explaining how the SBA can help a small business get started and succeed.

   _____

   _____

   _____

Chapter 19

Chapter 19 Financing Your Business
Case Study Activity
Animation Technology

Directions Read the *BusinessWeek* Case Study feature in this chapter. Then study the graphs and answer the questions that follow.

Top 10 Digital Music Markets Worldwide		Online	Mobile
1	USA	67%	33%
2	Japan	9%	91%
3	UK	71%	29%
4	South Korea	63%	37%
5	Germany	69%	31%
6	France	39%	61%
7	Canada	58%	42%
8	Australia	59%	41%
9	China	27%	73%
10	Italy	44%	56%

Source: IFPI, based on first half 2007 industry revenues.

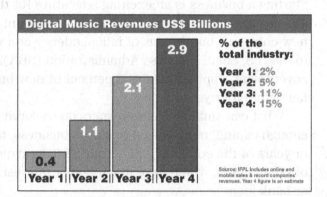

Digital Music Revenues US$ Billions

Year 1: 0.4   Year 2: 1.1   Year 3: 2.1   Year 4: 2.9

% of the total industry:
Year 1: 2%
Year 2: 5%
Year 3: 11%
Year 4: 15%

Source: IFPI. Includes online and mobile sales & record companies' revenues. Year 4 figure is an estimate

1. List the countries where digital music is downloaded onto mobile phones more often than onto computers.

   _____

   _____

2. By how much did digital music revenues increase between Year 3 and Year 4?

   _____

   _____

3. Which country has the largest percentage of revenue from the mobile market?

   _____

   _____

4. From the second graph, what are two general trends in digital music sales?

   _____

   _____

Chapter 19 Financing Your Business

Test Prep
True-False Tests

Directions Take the practice test below. Circle *T* for true or *F* for false. Rewrite false statements so that they are true.

1. Operating capital is the amount of cash you need to carry on your daily operations to ensure that the business makes a profit.   T   F

   _____

   _____

2. To accurately figure how much your start-up costs will be, you will need to talk to suppliers, vendors, manufacturers, distributors, and others in your industry.   T   F

   _____

   _____

3. A "tombstone" is a statement about the failure of the company.   T   F

   _____

   _____

4. The "red herring" is a prospectus that you must file with the SEC.   T   F

   _____

   _____

5. Capital expenditures must be included in your start-up costs.   T   F

   _____

   _____

6. The best way to find a venture capitalist is through an introduction from someone who knows the VC.   T   F

   _____

   _____

7. The five Cs that bankers rely on to accept a loan applicant are: character, capacity, capital, collateral, and control.   T   F

   _____

   _____

Chapter 19

Chapter 20 Accounting and Financial Reporting

Note Taking

Directions As you read, write notes, facts, and main ideas in the note-taking column. Write key words and short phrases in the cues column. Then summarize the section in the summary box.

Cues	Note Taking
	FINANCIAL RECORDKEEPING
• GAAP	• GAAP: "generally accepted accounting principles"
• income statement	**PREPARING FINANCIAL STATEMENTS**
	• Financial statements provide up-to-date business information. The income statement is a report of revenue, expenses, and net income or loss for an accounting period.
Summary	

Chapter 20

Chapter 20 Accounting and Financial Reporting
Section 20.1 Financial Record Keeping
Section Review: Identify

Directions Keeping track of what clients owe you is known as aging your accounts receivable. By aging your accounts receivable, you can determine who is slow in paying and who pays promptly. When using a manual system, the best way to do this is by setting up an aging table.

It is June 30, and you are getting ready to age your accounts receivable. Listed below are your clients, the date an invoice was generated, and the amount of the invoice. Using the table on the next page, mark the amount owed by each customer in the appropriate column. Then total the amounts due by "age" for your final answers. Note: In this business, an invoice is due 30 days from the date of its issuance.

Client	Date of Invoice	Amount of Invoice
A	May 28	$ 63.57
B	April 17	22.15
C	March 10	92.18
D	January 5	57.63
E	April 20	117.32
F	May 3	15.16
G	April 23	19.83
H	May 15	25.00
I	April 6	32.93
J	February 3	56.65
K	June 15	67.50
L	January 29	88.98
M	March 16	93.73
N	April 18	.17.62
O	March 20	31.93
P	May 20	.87.20
Q	February 20	76.30
R	April 2	91.73
S	March 3	18.20
T	June 2	27.63
U	May 21	.32.90
V	March 11	41.73
W	April 16	48.23
X	January 20	56.30
Y	March 14	11.25
Z	June 14	70.63

Continued on next page

Aging Table

Client	Not Due	1–30 Days Past Due	31–60 Days Past Due	61-90 Days Past Due	Over 90 Days
A					
B					
C					
D					
E					
F					
G					
H					
I					
J					
K					
L					
M					
N					
O					
P					
Q					
R					
S					
T					
U					
V					
W					
X					
Y					
Z					
Total					
Percent of Total					

Chapter 20 Accounting and Financial Reporting
Section 20.2 Preparing Financial Statements
Section Review: Record

Directions How much money will you need to start a business? How much money do you have? Where will you find money? How will you be evaluated by a banker? All of these questions must be answered as you prepare to finance your business. As you learned, the main source of start-up capital for new businesses is an entrepreneur's personal savings. If this is the case, then you need to spend some time analyzing your personal financial position. Even if you decide to see potential investors or go to a bank, the lender will be interested in studying your financial position.

Below is an example of a very simple personal financial statement prepared for this purpose. Notice that it follows the basic format of a balance sheet in that total assets equal total liabilities plus net worth (the personal equivalent of owner's equity). Follow this format to complete the simple form on the following page. Complete as much of it as you can. Since the two-page form is so comprehensive, you may find yourself unable to complete many of its entries. You can probably use it, however, to construct your own statement, one that falls midway between the two extremes presented here.

PERSONAL FINANCIAL STATEMENT
Steven J. Kent
Statement of Financial Condition
August 23, 201—

Assets

Cash in checking accounts	$1,200	
Cash in savings accounts	5,000	
Personal property and furnishings	850	
Total Assets		$7,050

Liabilities

Short-term loans	$500	
Miscellaneous charge accounts	300	
Truck loan	5,000	
Total Liabilities		5,800

Net Worth

Steven J. Kent		$1,250

Continued on next page

Chapter 20

STATEMENT OF FINANCIAL CONDITION

_____

(YOUR NAME)

Dated _____

Assets

Cash in checking accounts	$ _____
Cash in savings accounts	$ _____
Personal property and furnishings	$ _____
Total Assets	$ _____

Liabilities

Short-term loans	$ _____
Miscellaneous charge accounts	$ _____
Other	$ _____
Total Liabilities	$ _____

Net Worth

Your name	$ _____

Continued on next page

Chapter 20

PERSONAL FINANCIAL STATEMENT

Financial Statement as of _____ 20_____. If you are seeking credit jointly with your spouse, or if you are relying on your spouse's assets or income in requesting credit, this statement should reflect the financial condition of your spouse as well as your own financial condition.

APPLICANT'S NAME		DATE OF BIRTH	CO-APPLICANT (INCLUDES APPLICANT'S SPOUSE)		DATE OF BIRTH
RESIDENCE ADDRESS			RELATIONSHIP TO APPLICANT		
			RESIDENCE ADDRESS		
EMPLOYED BY			EMPLOYED BY		
BUSINESS ADDRESS		TELEPHONE NO.	BUSINESS ADDRESS		TELEPHONE NO.
KIND OF BUSINESS	POSITION	HOW LONG THERE	KIND OF BUSINESS	POSITION	HOW LONG THERE
FIXED OR AVERAGE SALARY $ PER	Income you may receive from alimony, child support, or maintenance payments need not be revealed if you do not choose to disclose such income in applying for credit		FIXED OR AVERAGE SALARY $ PER	Income you may receive from alimony, child support, or maintenance payments need not be revealed if you do not choose to disclose such income in applying for credit	
AMOUNT OF OTHER INCOME $	SOURCE — RENTALS, DIVIDENDS, ETC.		AMOUNT OF OTHER INCOME $	SOURCE — RENTALS, DIVIDENDS, ETC.	

NAME OF BANK WHERE YOU DEPOSIT		BRANCH	SAVINGS	CHECKING

ASSETS		IN EVEN DOLLARS	LIABILITIES		IN EVEN DOLLARS
CASH ON HAND & IN BANKS			NOTES PAYABLE TO BANKS	(SCHED. D)	
MARKETABLE SECURITIES	(SCHED. A)		NOTES PAYABLE TO OTHERS	(SCHED. D)	
NON-MARKETABLE SECURITIES	(SCHED. B)		ACCOUNTS PAYABLE	(SCHED. E)	
RESTRICTED OR CONTROL STOCK	(SCHED. B)		REAL ESTATE MORTGAGES	(SCHED. F)	
SECURITIES HELD BY BROKERS IN MARGIN ACCTS.			DUE TO BROKERS		
REAL ESTATE	(SCHED. F)		UNPAID INCOME TAX		
NOTES RECEIVABLE	(SCHED. G)		CREDIT CARDS (OUTSTANDING BALANCE)		
ACCOUNTS RECEIVABLE	(SCHED. G)		OTHER LIABILITIES (ITEMIZE)		
CASH VALUE — LIFE INSURANCE	(SCHED. C)				
AUTOS YEAR MAKE					
YEAR MAKE					
HOUSEHOLD GOODS					
JEWELRY					
ASSETS HELD IN TRUST					
OTHER ASSETS (ITEMIZE)			(SEE SCHEDULE H FOR CONTINGENT LIAB.)		
			TOTAL LIABILITIES		
			NET WORTH		
TOTAL ASSETS			TOTAL LIABILITIES AND NET WORTH		

DETAILS RELATIVE TO ASSETS AND LIABILITIES (IF SPACE IS INSUFFICIENT, ATTACH SUPPLEMENTAL LIST)

(A) MARKETABLE SECURITIES — LIST	TITLE IN NAME OF	PREF. OR COMMON	NO. OF SHARES	MARKET VALUE	SHARES PLEDGED	WHERE PLEDGED

The Ohio laws against discrimination require that all creditors make credit equally available to all creditworthy customers, and that credit reporting agencies maintain separate credit histories on each individual upon request. The Ohio Civil Rights Commission administers compliance with this law.

This financial statement is submitted for the purpose of procuring, establishing and maintaining credit with you in behalf of the undersigned or persons, firms or corporations in whose behalf the undersigned may either severally or jointly with others execute a guaranty in your favor. The undersigned warrants that this financial statement is true and correct and authorizes the Bank to obtain information concerning any statements made herin.

DATE THIS STATEMENT SIGNED:_____ SIGNED: _____

DATE THIS STATEMENT SIGNED:_____ SIGNED: _____

Continued on next page

Chapter 20

(B) NON-MARKETABLE SECURITIES — LIST (INCLUDING RESTRICTED OR CONTROL STOCK)	TITLE IN NAME OF	SHARES OWNED	SHARES ISSUED	BOOK OR OTHER VALUE	SHARES PLEDGED	WHERE PLEDGED

(C) LIFE INSURANCE COMPANY	OWNER	FACE AMOUNT	BENEFICIARY	KIND OF INSURANCE	CASH VALUE	AMOUNT OF POLICY OR LOAN

(D) NOTES PAYABLE — TO	AMOUNT	DATE MADE	DATE DUE	REPAYMENT SCHEDULE	SECURED OR ENDORSED BY

(E) ACCOUNTS PAYABLE — TO	AMOUNT	DATE MADE	DATE DUE	FOR WHAT

(F) REAL ESTATE — DESCRIPTION	LOCATION	TITLE IN WHOSE NAME	AMOUNT OF INSURANCE
1.			
2.			
3.			
4.			
5.			
6.			

DATE ACQUIRED	ORIGINAL COST	1ST MORTGAGE BALANCE	2ND MORTGAGE BALANCE	IST MORTGAGE PAYMENT	2ND MORTGAGE PAYMENT	REAL ESTATE TAXES	RENTALS REC'D DURING LAST CALENDAR YEAR
1.							
2.							
3.							
4.							
5.							
6.							

MORTGAGE HOLDERS — FIRST MORTGAGE HELD BY	SECOND MORTGAGE HELD BY
PARCEL NO.1	
PARCEL NO.2	
PARCEL NO.3	
PARCEL NO.4	
PARCEL NO.5	
PARCEL NO.6	

(G) ACCTS. & NOTES RECEIVABLE — FROM	AMT. DUE	MATURITY	REPAYMENT SCHEDULE	SECURITY — IF ANY

(H) CONTINGENT LIABILITIES	(DEBTOR)	AMOUNT
AS ENDORSER, CO-MAKER OR GUARANTOR		
ON LEASES OR CONTRACTS		
OTHER		

REMARKS

Chapter 20

Chapter 20 Accounting and Financial Reporting

Software Activity
Spreadsheet Application

Directions The objective of this activity is to prepare a profit and loss statement.

A profit and loss statement compares revenues and expenses over a specific period of time to determine if a business has made a profit. Components on most profit and loss statements include net sales, cost of goods sold, gross margin, operating expenses, and net income after taxes. Each of these components is often shown as a percent of sales on the profit and loss statement.

Practice Situation The printout below shows components of a typical profit and loss statement. You have been provided with net sales, cost of goods sold, and specific expenses. To complete the profit and loss statement, you will need to calculate the gross margin, total operating expenses, and net income before taxes. Next, calculate the percent of sales that each component represents.

ACME MODEL COMPANY Profit and Loss Statement January 1–December 31		
		Percent of Sales
Net Sales	$493,148	100%
Cost of Goods Sold	$291,262	_____
GROSS MARGIN		_____
Operating Expenses:		
Salaries	$83,138	_____
Utilities	$6,950	_____
Depreciation	$10,050	_____
Rent	$32,000	_____
Building Services	$4,920	_____
Insurance	$4,000	_____
Interest	$2,646	_____
Office and Supplies	$6,550	_____
Sales Promotion	$11,000	_____
Taxes and Licenses	$6,480	_____
Maintenance	$1,610	_____
Delivery	$5,848	_____
Miscellaneous	$1,750	_____
TOTAL OPERATING EXPENSES		_____
NET INCOME BEFORE TAXES		_____

Continued on next page

Chapter 20

Spreadsheet Directions

1. Start your spreadsheet software program.

2. Re-create the table from the previous page using your spreadsheet program.

3. Enter the appropriate formulas to calculate the following:

   • gross margin

   • total operating expenses

   • net income before taxes

4. Enter the formula for calculating the percent of sales for each of the components listed.

5. After completing your calculations, save your work.

6. Print out a copy of your work if your teacher has instructed you to do so.

7. Answer the following questions.

Interpreting Results

1. What was the net income before taxes for Acme Model Company?

   _____

   _____

2. What percent of sales did net income before taxes represent?

   _____

   _____

Drawing Conclusions

3. What three general strategies could Acme Model Company use to increase its net income before taxes?

   _____

   _____

   _____

4. If Acme Model Company generates more sales next year, will profits increase?

   _____

   _____

   _____

Chapter 20

Name _____ Date _____ Class _____

Chapter 20 Accounting and Financial Reporting

Academic Integration Activity

Mathematics
Tracking Cash Flow

Directions An important part of record keeping is keeping track of how much cash you have on hand. This is done by reconciling the monthly bank statement you receive for your business's checking account. The reconciliation process is the same as that used for a personal checking account. The numbers may just be a little larger.

Below is a summary of information from a checking account statement and register (the handwritten record you keep of the checks you write and the deposits you make). Use the reconciliation form on the following page to find out if your check register and bank statement are in agreement. (In other words, do your checkbook and bank statement balances match?)

Statement Balance (Bank Balance)
$1,875.92

Outstanding Checks

#1803	5.39
1833	6.88
1851	25.73
1858	10.18
1863	125.73
1864	98.08
1869	327.33
1870	15.66
1871	32.93
1872	18.92
1873	6.57
1874	808.72

Outstanding Deposits
$ 319.57
1,429.38
319.57

Interest Earned
$ 32.73

Service Charges
$ 22.17

Register Balance (Checkbook Balance)
$2,477.88

Continued on next page

Name _____ Date _____ Class _____

Bank Reconciliation Statement

BANK RECONCILIATION WORKSHEET

ITEMS OUTSTANDING	
NUMBER	AMOUNT
TOTAL	

TO BALANCE YOUR ACCOUNT:

ENTER
the new balance shown on
your statement...$ _____

ADD
any deposits listed in your $ _____
register that are not shown $ _____
on your statement $ _____

                                    TOTAL $ _____
CALCULATE THE SUBTOTAL....................................$ _____

SUBTRACT
the total outstanding checks
and withdrawals from the
chart at left ....$ _____

CALCULATE THE ENDING BALANCE
which should be the same as
the current balance in your
check register ....$ [_____]

Is your check register in agreement with the bank statement?

_____

_____

_____

_____

_____

Name _____ Date _____ Class _____

Chapter 20 Accounting and Financial Reporting
Academic Integration Activity

Social Studies
Accounting Ethics

Directions Read the article about ethics in accounting, then answer the questions.

ETHICS

In practice, *ethics* refers to a set of basic principles that can guide a person who is facing a question of whether a particular act is right or wrong. Honesty, trust, respect, and fairness are among the policies and practices that are a part of a company's core values. Most companies have a defined code of ethics that everyone, from owner to entry-level employee, are expected to follow.

The U.S. financial industry has been affected in recent years by high-profile examples of unethical behavior by accounting firms, including all of the "Big Four" major public accounting firms: Deloitte & Touche, Ernst & Young, KMPG, and Pricewaterhouse Cooper. These firms, hired to audit (evaluate) accounting records prepared by their corporate clients, admitted to or were accused of failing to prevent the publication of inaccurate financial reports. The reports gave investors false impressions about companies' financial standing and investment risks.

The American Institute of Certified Public Accountants (AICPA), the national, professional organization for certified public accountants, has strongly defended its membership and the accounting profession. AICPA members voluntarily accept the standards described in the AICPA Code of Professional Conduct.

---

1. Find the Web site for AICPA. From the home page, click on "About the AICPA," then click on "AICPA Mission." What is AICPA's mission?

_____

_____

_____

_____

2. Return to the home page and type "Ethics Decision Tree" in the search engine. Follow steps to open the Ethics Decision Tree. Study the document, then write a few sentences summarizing the first two paragraphs of the introduction.

_____

_____

_____

_____

Chapter 20 Accounting and Financial Reporting

Case Study Activity

Operating Expenses

Directions Read the *BusinessWeek* Case Study feature in this chapter. Then read the scenarios and complete the tables.

Your business must keep accurate records of all its operating expenses. This information can be used to complete the income statement, determine net income or less, and to plan future spending. You may calculate the percentage of each expense by comparing it to your total expense. Use this formula:

Percentage of Total = Particular Expense ÷ Total Expenses.

1. Charlestown Nursery had the following expenses last year. Find the total. Find what percentage each expense is of the total.

Item	Amount	Percentage of Total
Payroll	$534,429	
Advertising	42,900	
Equipment	12,249	
Property payment/taxes	34,218	
Supplies/flowers	355,198	
Insurance	15,231	
Utilities	17,360	
Total	_____	_____

2. This year, the nursery's goals were to lower total operating expenses to under $950,000, bring payroll to under 50 percent of total expenses, and get supplies/flowers to under one-third of total expenses. Find the total. Find what percentage each expense is of total.

Item	Amount	Percentage of Total
Payroll	$502,320	
Advertising	43,500	
Equipment	15,100	
Property payment/taxes	34,859	
Supplies/flowers	326,206	
Insurance	16,040	
Utilities	14,925	
Total	_____	_____

Chapter 20 Accounting and Financial Reporting

 **Test Prep**
Thinking Strategies

Directions Read the thinking strategies, then use the information from the previous page to answer the questions.

THINKING STRATEGIES
• Look for patterns and relationships among the ideas in the material. • Make connections between ideas. Find connections even when the ideas seem to contrast. • Think in metaphors. Link separate ideas together. • Prepare yourself for change. Be ready for the unexpected.

1. Which is the largest operating expense?

   _____

2. Which expenses increased from the previous year?

   _____

3. Which expenses decreased as percentage of total?

   _____

4. How many of Charlestown Nursery's goals were accomplished?

   _____

5. By what amount over or under the target goal were the nursery's total expenses?

   _____

6. By what percentage over or under the target goal were the expenses for supplies and flowers?

   _____

Chapter 20

Chapter 21 Financial Management

 Note Taking

Directions As you read, write notes, facts, and main ideas in the note-taking column. Write key words and short phrases in the cues column. Then summarize the section in the summary box.

Cues	Note Taking
	ANALYZING YOUR FINANCES
• comparative financial statement: compares data in two different accounting periods	• Primary financial statements: income statement (P&L), balance sheet
	MANAGING YOUR FINANCES
• variable expenses: change per units produced	• Planning for profits includes forecasting sales, evaluating profit potential, controlling costs, and budgeting.
Summary	

Chapter 21   Financial Management
Section 21.1 Analyzing Your Finances
Section Review: Analyze

Directions One of the ways businesses analyze their financial condition is by comparing certain numbers on a balance sheet or income statement. This analysis to compare the relationship between the two figures is called ratio analysis.

Based on the guidelines presented in the chapter, calculate the following ratios and state what the ratio tells about the business. If you are unable to determine from the information given, write *Cannot determine*. (Note: Round to the second decimal place.)

1. Calculate the current ratio based on the following information:

   Current assets $650,000
   Current liabilities $400,000
   Current ratio =   _____

   _____
   _____
   _____
   _____
   _____
   _____
   _____

2. Calculate the current ratio based on the following information:

   Current assets $850,000
   Current liabilities $325,000
   Current ratio =   _____

   _____
   _____
   _____
   _____
   _____
   _____
   _____

Continued on next page

3. Calculate the debt ratio based on the following information:

Current assets	$650,000
Current liabilities	$400,000
Current ratio =	_____

_____

_____

_____

_____

_____

_____

4. Calculate the net profit on sales based on the following information:

Current net income	$65,000
Current sales	$415,000
Current ratio =	_____

_____

_____

_____

_____

_____

_____

_____

5. Calculate the operating ratio for rent based on the following information:

Current assets	$650,000
Current liabilities	$400,000
Current ratio =	_____

_____

_____

_____

_____

_____

_____

Chapter 21 Financial Management
Section 21.2 Managing Your Finances
Section Review: Interpret

Directions Read the scenario about cash flow. Study the cash flow diagram below and draw your own diagram on the next page. Then answer the questions that follow.

Simone owns a small business that sells wreaths and wall hangings made of herbs and other natural materials. She has two full-time employees and hires part-time employees for the holiday seasons. During her peak time, payroll and benefits amount to $2,100 per month.

She sells to customers by direct mail and has had a very good year. She has averaged 500 units a month at an average selling price of $30 per unit. During the month of December, she expects to sell 1,000 units. Her gross sales for the year will be $195,000.

Her cash on hand at the beginning of December is $20,000. She incurred inventory expenses in November totaling $15,000, which are payable in December. In December she anticipates cash payments of $12,000 for merchandise shipped and has $5,000 accounts receivable due. She will also have operating expenses totaling $6,000.

Everything looked steady until Simone began to project her cash flow into the month of January. In order to replenish inventory, she figures inventory expenses in January will be approximately $16,000. This news does not make Simone happy.

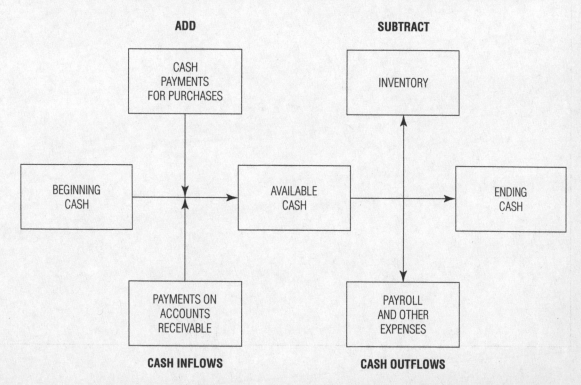

Continued on next page

Cash Flow Diagram

1. What is the available cash for December?

_____

_____

2. What is the ending cash balance as of December 31?

_____

_____

3. Why might Simone be unhappy?

_____

_____

_____

_____

_____

_____

_____

4. What should Simone do to manage her pending cash flow difficulty? What does she need to do to lessen the possibility that this situation will reoccur?

_____

_____

_____

_____

_____

_____

_____

_____

Chapter 21 Financial Management

 Software Activity
Spreadsheet Application

Directions The objective of this activity is to calculate the break-even point.

At one point or another, many entrepreneurs must decide whether or not to add new products as a way of increasing profits for the firm. However, they must remember that every change has a cost, and sometimes that cost is more than the change is worth. Before deciding to invest in a change, entrepreneurs should evaluate profit potential by using a break-even analysis.

Practice Situation

The printout below illustrates a product that you are considering to add to inventory. Fixed and Variable Costs are given in relation to five suggested selling prices. Calculate the break-even point in units for each of the selling prices given.

Fixed Costs	Variable Costs	Selling Price	Break-Even Point
$1,000	$7.50	$13	
$1,000	$7.50	$14	
$1,000	$7.50	$15	
$1,000	$7.50	$16	
$1,000	$7.50	$17	

Spreadsheet Directions

1. Start your spreadsheet software program.

2. Re-create the table above using your spreadsheet program.

3. For the selling price of $13, input the formula to calculate the break-even point. Copy this formula for the other four products.

4. After completing your calculations, save your work.

5. Print out a copy of your work if your teacher has instructed you to do so.

6. Answer the following questions.

Interpreting Results

1. At which selling price would you have the lowest break-even point?

   _____

   _____

   _____

2. Should you price the product at $17 if it is added to your inventory?

   _____

   _____

   _____

   _____

Drawing Conclusions

3. You decide to add the product to your inventory and set a retail price of $17. Will you be guaranteed a profit?

   _____

   _____

   _____

   _____

   _____

   _____

   _____

   _____

   _____

   _____

Chapter 21 Financial Management

Academic Integration Activity

 Mathematics
Break-Even Analysis

A break-even analysis tells you how many units of product must be sold to cover the cost of production. Any item sold beyond the break-even point results in a profit for your business. To answer the questions below, use the following formula:

Fixed Cost ÷ (Selling Price − Variable Cost) = Break-Even Point

Directions Complete the table. Find the break-even point to the nearest whole number.

	Item	Fixed Cost	Selling Price per Unit	Variable Costs per Unit	Break-Even Point in Units
1.	Keychain	$75,000	$2.19	$0.99	
2.	Soap Dish	$140,000	$0.89	$0.19	
3.	Bicycle	$2,225,000	$229.99	$66.19	
4.	Hi-Def TV	$350,000,000	$1,117.79	$349.81	

Directions Find the break-even point to the nearest whole number.

5. The Johnstown Company manufactures porcelain figurines. The fixed costs of the product total $124,362.88. The average selling price per figurine is $210.10. The variable cost per bowl is $54.65. What is the break-even point in number of figurines?

_____

6. Whisk-Off dog collar is produced by Pet Mart. The company has fixed costs of $2,000,000 in the manufacture of the collar. The selling price of each collar is $9.95. The variable cost per collar is $7.55. What is the break-even point in number of collars?

_____

_____

7. Toby Toy manufactures teddy bears. The company has fixed costs of $232,552 in the production of the bears. The selling price of each bear is $19.16. The variable cost per bear is $15.15. What is the break-even point in number of bears?

_____

_____

8. Your company produces In-A-Stick glue in 8-oz tubes. The fixed costs for the production of the glue tubes are $477,999.50. The variable cost per tube is $0.38. The selling price is $1.16 per tube. What is the break-even point in tubes of In-A-Stick glue?

_____

_____

Chapter 21 Financial Management

Academic Integration Activity

Social Studies
Writing Collection Correspondence

Directions In Chapter 20, you learned that a close follow-up makes it easier to collect past due accounts. You also learned the sequence of steps involved in collecting those accounts.

Each of the following situations calls for engaging in one of the steps in collecting a past due account. Using your general knowledge and the guidelines provided, prepare the necessary correspondence or plan to follow up the past due account.

Situation 1: The account of Joel Brophy is over 30 days past due. Three days after the due date, you sent a payment notice indicating a 5 percent late charge would be assessed if the payment was not made before today.

Follow-Up: Write a first letter for payment to the customer. In the body of your letter explain why you are writing and request payment or contact by (_____). Keep this letter short and to the point.

_____

_____

_____

_____

_____

_____

_____

_____

_____

_____

_____

_____

_____

_____

_____

Continued on next page

Chapter 21

Situation 2: You have sent out a notice and a first letter to Allen Parker. Because of the extension time given in your notice and the first letter, the account is now actually (_____) days past due.

Follow-Up: Write second letter for payment to the customer. In this letter, review the terms of the contract and note that no payment or contact has been received to date. Emphasize that the situation must be resolved by (_____). This letter should be more detailed and firm than the first.

_____

_____

_____

_____

_____

_____

_____

Situation 3: Jill Montero's account was past due in the 30-day category when you did your last aging. Since you pulled the account, you have sent a notice and two letters to her and had no response.

Follow-Up: Plan a phone call to follow up this account. Include a brief description of each step of the call in your plan. Note: Since the next payment will be due, it may be useful to discuss that payment as well.

_____

_____

_____

_____

_____

_____

_____

_____

_____

_____

Situation 4: Robert Spark's account is now 60 days past-due. The customer did not respond to your notice or two letters. Although he promised to make payment as a result of your phone call, payment was not made. The account has a high balance.

Follow-Up: It is time to make a personal call on a past-due customer. Identify what preparations you would make for the visit. List the points you would cover at the beginning of the meeting. Describe the process you would use to help the customer solve the problem. Predetermine an acceptable situation.

_____

_____

_____

_____

_____

_____

_____

_____

_____

_____

_____

_____

Situation 5: The customer in Situation 4 has not done what he agreed to at the end of your meeting.

Follow-Up: Review your options. What additional internal options do you have? How far will you go with the customer before going to external options? What external options are appropriate for your business? What is your decision regarding the next step? What is the rationale for your decision?

_____

_____

_____

_____

_____

_____

_____

_____

Chapter 21 Financial Management
Case Study Activity
Personal Finance

Directions Read the *BusinessWeek* Case Study feature in this chapter. Then read the scenario and complete the table.

Making a budget and sticking to it is one of the best ways to manage money responsibly. Assume the individual budget below is yours. Fill in the missing data and use the budget to answer the questions that follow.

Monthly Fixed (Unchanging) Expenses	
Mortgage payments	$ 950.00
Car payments	225.00
Television payments	60.00
Savings	100.00
Set aside for emergencies	50.00
Total	
Annual Fixed Expenses	
Insurance Premiums	
Medical/Dental	$ 1,200.00
Car	660.00
Life	1,020.00
Homeowners	600.00
Charitable Contributions	300.00
Vehicle Registration	200.00
Total	
Monthly Share	
Monthly Living Expenses	
Food	$ 500.00
Clothing	85.00
Newspapers & magazines	20.00
Recreation & entertainment	100.00
Cell phone plan	100.00
Household operation	
Electricity and Gas	135.00
Telephone (land line)	40.00
Water	25.00

Automobile	
Gas and oil	275.00
Repair and maintenance	30.00
Bus and subway fares	40.00
Other expenses	150.00
Total	
Income (take-home pay)	**$3,550.00**
Total Expenses **(Monthly Fixed + Annual Fixed [Monthly Share] + Living Expenses)**	

1. Which are the two largest monthly expenses in your budget?

_____

_____

_____

_____

2. What percent of total monthly expenses does each expense category represent? Divide each expense category by total expenses.

Monthly Fixed Expenses _____

Monthly Share of Annual Fixed Expenses _____

Monthly Living Expenses _____

3. Do you have a positive or negative net income? By how much? Subtract Total Expenses from Income (take-home pay).

_____

_____

_____

_____

4. You want to increase the money you save, so you can take a two-week vacation next summer. How might you be able to adjust your budget in order to afford the vacation?

_____

_____

_____

_____

Chapter 21 Financial Management

Test Prep
Effective Test Preparation

Directions Read the tips for effective test preparation, then choose the word or phrase that best completes the following sentences.

EFFECTIVE TEST PREPARATION
• Stay current on your reading and assignments. It is harder to catch up once you lag behind.
• Learn the material as you study it in class. Be sure to ask your teacher to explain any information you do not understand.
• Review the materials on a regular basis.
• Practice taking the test with classmates before test day. Quiz each other on the material that will be on the test.

1. The major advantage of extending credit is that
   a. selling by telephone and Internet is easier.
   b. credit account records are useful for marketing and market research.
   c. sales volume is increased.
   d. closer relationships can be built with customers by making purchases easier.

2. Which of the following use ratio analysis to determine the financial strength, activity, or bill-paying ability of the business?
   a. owners
   b. lenders
   c. creditors
   d. all of the above

3. Which of the following statements is true about accountants?
   a. They make business decisions.
   b. They prepare financial records.
   c. They interpret financial records.
   d. all of the above

4. A quick ratio is calculated using amounts found on
   a. the balance sheet.
   b. the sales report.
   c. the income statement.
   d. the cash budget.

5. The reason you evaluate and adjust your profit planning is to
   a. obtain more credit from lenders.
   b. improve your profit picture.
   c. decrease theft.
   d. increase inventory.

Chapter 22 Risk Management

 Note Taking

Directions As you read, write notes, facts, and main ideas in the note-taking column. Write key words and short phrases in the cues column. Then summarize the section in the summary box.

Cues	Note Taking
• risk: the possibility of loss or injury	**IDENTIFYING BUSINESS RISKS** • Risk is inevitable in business. Speculative risk: taking a risk for profit or loss. Pure risk: threat of loss without any chance of gain.
• premium	**DEALING WITH RISK** • Risk management process: 1. Identify risks; 2. Estimate potential losses from risks; 3. Determine best ways to deal with risks.
Summary	

Chapter 22 Risk Management
Section 22.1 Identifying Business Risks
Section Review: Connect

Directions Lisa and Phil have decided to expand their catering business to accommodate larger orders and offer in-home preparation. However, this expansion will mean hiring additional help and dealing with increased business risks. The services the catering business will offer include planning and pre-event preparation, transportation of equipment and personnel to events, and on-site preparation of food. Events will include business functions and private parties.

Until now, Lisa and Phil have not had to be too concerned with risks. They were the only ones involved in the business, and most of their clients were friends. But now they have to consider risk management. Help them by providing answers to the questions below. Rely on information presented in the chapter, as well as your own entrepreneurial instincts.

1. What are the risks you can identify for Lisa and Phil? Try to think of at least 10.

   a. _____

   b. _____

   c. _____

   d. _____

   e. _____

   f. _____

   g. _____

   h. _____

   i. _____

   j. _____

2. What advice would you give Lisa and Phil about developing a risk management plan? (Note: The plan should cover all of the risks you identified in question 1 and provide recommendations for dealing with them.)

   _____

   _____

   _____

   _____

   _____

   _____

   _____

Chapter 22 Risk Management
Section 22.2 Dealing with Risk
Section Review: Plan

Directions One of the many issues you will face as an entrepreneur is how to protect your business from various kinds of risk. Chapter 22 discusses four separate strategies for dealing with risk—**avoidance, reduction, transfer, and retention.**

   Each of the examples below falls into one of these categories. Assume that you are the entrepreneur in each instance, and decide which form of risk management is being used. Write your answers in the appropriate blanks.

1. _____ You decide to purchase business interruption insurance.

2. _____ You put flood lamps at each exterior corner of the store.

3. _____ You hire someone to scrape the parking lot and shovel the entryway when snow falls.

4. _____ You teach your stockroom employees how to lift heavy boxes so as to avoid back injuries.

5. _____ You choose not to carry a line of products that appears to be especially easy to shoplift.

6. _____ You have a qualified person check the fire extinguishers in your place of business each month.

7. _____ You purchase fire insurance.

8. _____ You pay workers' compensation each month.

9. _____ You save a percentage of profits each month to guard against short-term economic downturns.

10. _____ You install electronic sensors to discourage shoplifting.

11. _____ You have a silent alarm system installed that signals the nearest police station.

12. _____ You instruct employees in the use of potentially dangerous equipment.

13. _____ You move your store from an isolated corner to a busy mall.

14. _____ You hold employee meetings to discuss ways of reducing accidents.

Continued on next page

Chapter 22

15. _____ In response to what you believe to be exorbitantly high premiums, you decide to drop your property insurance and self-insure instead.

16. _____ You bond your employees who handle cash.

17. _____ You educate your employees in the storage and handling of hazardous substances they must use on the job.

18. _____ When it rains, you place nonskid floor mats in the entryways of your business.

19. _____ You contract with a local security firm to patrol your business premises at night.

20. _____ You establish bonding insurance for your employees through your business.

21. _____ You provide your employees with first aid and CPR training.

22. _____ You add uninsured and underinsured motorists coverage to the policy you already have for your business's delivery vans.

23. _____ Because you cannot afford health insurance for yourself or your family, you make regular deposits to a bank account you maintain for coping with health care emergencies.

24. _____ You make regular payments to your state's workers' compensation plan.

25. _____ You elect not to make COD deliveries and advertise this fact by placing "Driver carries no cash" stickers on the windows of your delivery vans.

26. _____ You install an electronic credit authorizer by your cash register.

27. _____ You place signs at key points around the sales floor and near exits, indicating that shoplifters will be prosecuted to the full limits of the law.

28. _____ You provide your employees with safety gear and see that it is used routinely and properly.

Chapter 22 Risk Management

Software Activity
PowerPoint Application

Directions The objective of this activity is to identify risks faced by a business and present a risk reduction program.

All entrepreneurs face risk. Business owners must be aware of all the risks they face and develop programs of risk reduction or risk transfer. In addition, there may be situations where the entrepreneur will accept risk. This situation is known as risk retention. As a business owner, you will want your employees to be aware of the risks faced by your firm. In addition, you will want to alert them to activities that can reduce losses from these risks.

Practice Situation

Select a business that you may be interested in starting in the future. Identify all the risks faced by that business. Then, make a list of activities that the owner of that business could implement to reduce losses from these risks. In other words, you will be developing a risk reduction program.

Create a slide presentation that lists the types of risks faced by the business you investigated. The next slides should include a list of risk prevention activities that could be used in a training session with employees. Use several different types of slides (as shown below) to present your findings. One should be a title slide and at least one of the slides should include clip art.

Type of Business

Types of Risks
- Risk One
- Risk Two
- Risk Three

Risk One Reduction
- Prevention Activities
- Employee Training

Continued on next page

PowerPoint Directions

1. Start your PowerPoint software program.

2. Based on the information you have collected, develop a minimum of six slides that will identify the risks faced by the business, and a list of risk reduction activities that could be used to lessen losses.

3. Save your work.

4. Print out a copy of your slides if your teacher has instructed you to do so.

5. Answer the following questions.

Interpreting Results

1. Why is it important for entrepreneurs to identify risks and develop risk reduction programs?

_____

_____

_____

_____

2. Present your slide presentation to your class. Were there risks that were common in all the presentations? Were there any risks that were unique to only one of the businesses presented?

_____

_____

_____

_____

_____

Drawing Conclusions

3. Why is it important for a business owner to present a risk reduction program to employees?

_____

_____

_____

_____

Chapter 22 Risk Management
Academic Integration Activity

English Language Arts
Writing Skills

Directions Fill in the graphic organizer.

Read the word.	Predict what the word means.	Write the dictionary definition of the word.
speculative		
negligence		
burglary		
robbery		
premium		
fidelity		
omissions		
compensation		

Chapter 22 Risk Management
Academic Integration Activity

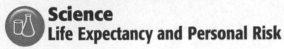

Science
Life Expectancy and Personal Risk

Directions Study the "U.S. Life Expectancy From Birth" table, then answer the questions.

U.S. LIFE EXPECTANCY FROM BIRTH

Year	Total	Male	Female
1900	47.3	46.3	48.3
1910	50.0	48.4	51.8
1920	54.1	53.6	54.6
1930	59.7	58.1	61.6
1940	62.9	60.8	65.2
1950	68.2	65.6	71.1
1960	69.7	66.6	73.1
1970	70.8	67.1	74.7
1980	73.7	70.0	77.5
1990	75.4	71.8	78.8
2000	77.5	74.8	80.1
2010	79.3	76.6	82.3

Source: U.S. Department of Health and Human Services, National Center for Health Statistics

1. When did life expectancy for both men and women first exceed 60 years? _____

_____

_____

2. In which year was the difference in life expectancy for men and women the least? What was the difference?

_____

_____

3. According to the data on the table, the total life expectancy has increased an average of 0.29 each year between 1900 and 2010. If this average is maintained, during which future year will total life expectancy reach age 80?

_____

_____

_____

_____

_____

_____

_____

4. Divide into small groups. Brainstorm a list of reasons why your group thinks life expectancy has steadily increased since 1900.

_____

_____

_____

_____

_____

_____

5. List three things you can do now to reduce personal risk and help ensure a longer life span.

_____

_____

_____

_____

_____

_____

_____

_____

Chapter 22 Risk Management
Case Study Activity
Personal Finance

Directions Read the *BusinessWeek* Case Study feature in this chapter of your textbook. Then read the article about insurance and use it to answer the questions that follow.

Florida is undoubtedly the state with the greatest exposure to hurricanes. Of the 158 hurricanes that hit the United States between 1900 and 1996, 47 hit Florida. But coastal states from Texas to Maine are all at risk for hurricanes, as is Hawaii. Prior to Hurricane Katrina, Hurricane Andrew in 1992 was the most expensive catastrophe in U.S. history with insured losses of $15.5 billion.

After fire, flooding is the most common and widespread of all natural disasters. Most communities in the United States have experienced flooding as a result of either spring rains, heavy thunderstorms, hurricanes, or winter snow thaws. To varying degrees, all areas are susceptible to flooding, but it is to be noted that 25% of flood claims occur in the low-to-moderate risk areas.

The risk of earthquakes is also widespread. Since 1990, earthquakes have occurred in 39 states and caused damage in all 50. Those who live west or just east of the Rockies are at most risk, but so are those people living in Alaska, New England, and in the New Madrid Fault area along the Mississippi. A total of 39 states have a medium to high potential for quakes, and roughly 90% of all Americans live in areas considered seismically active. However, the most earthquakes and the most costly earthquakes take place in California. Nine of the ten most costly earthquakes in the last century occurred in California: the Northridge earthquake in 1994 cost at least $12.5 billion dollars in insured losses and (prior to Hurricane Katrina) was the second most expensive natural disaster in U.S. history.

25% of all businesses that shut down after a natural disaster never re-open their doors.

Source: Cox Castle & Nicholson LLP

---

1. What is the most common natural disaster?
   a. fire
   b. hurricane
   c. earthquake
   d. flooding

2. Which state is *not* at risk for hurricanes?
   a. Hawaii
   b. Florida
   c. Missouri
   d. California

3. What do you think is the main implied (not stated but understood from context) message of the article?

   _____

   _____

   _____

Chapter 22 Risk Management

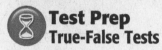

Test Prep
True-False Tests

Directions Circle **T** if the statement is true and **F** if the statement is false. If the statement is false, write a correct version on the line below.

1. Speculative risk involves the chance of either profit or loss.   **T F**

   _____

   _____

2. Large businesses are more likely to be the victims of crime than small   **T F**
   businesses.

   _____

   _____

3. Prosecution does not have an impact on the prevention of shoplifting.   **T F**

   _____

   _____

4. Establishing high standards for hiring is one of the keys to reducing   **T F**
   employee theft.

   _____

   _____

5. The best way to minimize the risk of burglary is through careful site selection. **T F**

   _____

   _____

6. It is the business owner's responsibility to protect employees and customers, **T F**
   which may mean letting the robber take what he or she wants.

   _____

   _____

7. Information provided by a electronic credit card authorizer is useful in   **T F**
   determining whether or not to accept a check.

   _____

   _____

Continued on next page

Chapter 22

8. Worms and trojan horses can be used to reduce the risk of a business owner becoming a victim of computer crime.   **T F**

_____

_____

9. Businesses cannot protect themselves against natural disasters.   **T F**

_____

_____

10. A company can be held responsible for an act of negligence.   **T F**

_____

_____

11. Holding meetings with employees to educate them regarding procedure for handling emergency situations is an example of risk transfer.   **T F**

_____

_____

12. A business can eliminate risks by practicing risk avoidance.   **T F**

_____

_____

13. Putting aside a sum of money each month to guard against future losses is a form of risk retention.   **T F**

_____

_____

14. Casualty insurance protects a business against losses from having to close for insurable reasons.   **T F**

_____

_____

Chapter 23 Making Your Business Grow

 Note Taking

Directions As you read, write notes, facts, and main ideas in the note-taking column. Write key words and short phrases in the cues column. Then summarize the section in the summary box.

Cues	Note Taking
	MAKING YOUR BUSINESS GROW
• market penetration	• Growth is natural development of a successful business start-up.
	CHALLENGES OF EXPANSION
• expansion	• Factors influencing business growth: market characteristics, innovation, delegation, vision, systems and controls

Summary

Chapter 23

Chapter 23 Making Your Business Grow
Section 23.1 Making Your Business Grow
Section Review: Comprehend

Directions Below is a case study written by Christopher Palmeri for *BusinessWeek* magazine. After you have read it, answer the questions that follow and determine how Trader Joe's made its business grow.

TRADER JOE'S

It began with plain, "Greek style" yogurt, which has a somewhat sharper taste than the traditional American kind. Then came the nonfat version and one mixed with honey. Soon, a cornucopia of new flavors appeared. Strawberry, fig, and the truly yummy apricot/mango blend. The cost: $1.29 container that is a little larger than a typical yogurt serving. That's how it is at Trader Joe's, where a trip to the supermarket is sort of a culinary adventure, a chance to discover something new, like apricot/mango Greek-style yogurt.

Of the ways to demonstrate customer service, Trader Joe's excels at one of the basics: delivering unique products at reasonable prices. The chain, which has about 300 stores in more than 20 states, has from its earliest days tried to bring unusual goods to a varied clientele. The strategy helped Trader Joe's rack up an impressive $6.5 billion in sales last year, according to the trade publication *Supermarket News*. "I do as much shopping as possible at Trader Joe's because of the prices," says Elizabeth Payne, an actress in Los Angeles.

Finding a Niche

Sandy Skrovan, who heads food store research at the consulting firm TNS Retail Forward, figures Trader Joe's generates sales in the neighborhood of $1,300 per square foot, double the supermarket industry average. Skrovan knows exactly how. She regularly shops for what she says is the widest variety of gluten-free foods at two company locations near her home in Columbus, Ohio. "When you think Trader Joe's you think of innovative products," she says. "That's what drives their model—return patronage and quality products at a fair price."

The strategy was born of desperation. In 1967 Joseph Coulombe owned a small chain of convenience stores in the Los Angeles area that were struggling to compete against a fast-growing newcomer named 7-Eleven. Coulombe decided to target a demographic now known as yuppies.

As the 1970s came, Coulombe was among the first to turn Southern California shoppers on to treats such as brie, wild rice, Dijon mustard, and Vermont maple syrup. Coulombe modeled his approach on that of Stew Leonard's, a Connecticut food merchant famous for carrying a limited assortment of quality products, and to that of Brooks Brothers, which sells only its own label suits. "We adopted a policy of not carrying anything we could not be outstanding in, in terms of price," Coulombe told *BusinessWeek* in a telephone interview. "It took us about five years because we had to create a whole new chain of logistics. We especially encouraged small businesses as vendors."

Private-Label Products

Today Trader Joe's carries about 2,000 products, versus 30,000 at a typical supermarket. About 80% of Trader Joe's goods are private label, compared with 16% for the rest of the supermarket industry. The chain doesn't carry familiar mass-market brands such as Coca-Cola, Nabisco, or Pampers. You will find just one kind of laundry detergent, the 'low-sudsing," biodegradable house brand. But there are 10 different kinds of hummus, starting at just $1.99.

Testing for many new products is done at company headquarters in the Los Angeles suburb of Monrovia, California. Staffers in the test kitchen ring a bell when new products are available so an employee tasting panel can sample.

Beyond that, though, the company does not like to talk about itself or its private-label suppliers. That hush-hush strategy is a two-way street. "Their suppliers simply don't talk to anyone about the company," says W. Frank Dell, a food industry consultant in Stamford, Conn. "They love the company. They are great to work with and pay their bills on time. They don't tell the outside world they have Trader Joe's as a customer." Other supermarket chains such as Kroger and Safeway have caught on to the private-label strategy, offering more prepared and organic foods. But Trader Joe's still manages to keep things fresh, introducing limited runs of Candy Cane Joe-Joe's cookies at holiday time that look like Oreos but taste like Girl Scouts' Thin Mints. "They're like a shark; they have to keep moving," says Len Lewis, who wrote a book, *The Trader Joe's Adventure*, about the company. "But they are very good at it, and now they have companies coming to them with new products."

Shopping at Trader Joe's isn't always a bowl of cherries. Parking at their urban locations is usually a challenge. Since the stores tend to be on the small side—less than 15,000 square feet versus 50,000 or more for conventional supermarkets—the lines can get long and the space cramped, especially on weekend afternoons.

Satisfied Workers

That's where another distinctive feature of Trader Joe's comes into play, its cheerful employees. Coulombe says he tried from the start to make Trader Joe's a place where people would enjoy coming to shop. Inspired by a trip to the Caribbean, he sought to make a shopping excursion resemble a vacation. Employees wear Hawaiian shirts, hand out food and drink samples from little tasting huts, and employ nautical terminology. Store managers are called captains, for example; assistant managers are known as first mates. The stores themselves look rustic, covered with cedar plank walls, for example, and hand-painted signs.

Ask a Trader Joe's employee about a product and he will practically sprint down the aisle, grab a bag of whatever you had questions about, and join you in a taste test. And returns? No questions asked, even if the goods have been opened and you simply didn't like the product. "The people who work there are just wonderful," says Ruth Leibowitz, a dance instructor from Ridgefield, Conn., who watched a Trader Joe's clerk dart to find her a bottle of the house brand (Trader Zen) ibuprofen during a recent trip.

Continued on next page

Chapter 23

Coulombe also wanted to make sure his employees were paid fairly, instituting a policy in the 1960s that full-time employees had to make at least the median household income for their communities—an average of $7,000 a year at the time, $48,000 today. Store captains, almost all of whom are promoted from within, can make six figures annually. Trader Joes also allows part-timers to earn health-care benefits, a feature that makes the store a haven for artists, musicians, and other creative types who wouldn't normally seek supermarket jobs.

A Successful Formula

Now 77 and retired, Coulombe sold Trader Joe's in 1979 to privately held German supermarket giant Aldi. The German owners have let the chain run more or less autonomously, keeping many of the original strategies in place.

Unlike most supermarkets, for example, Trader Joe's doesn't accept coupons, collect customer shopping info from loyalty cards, or feature weekly sales. Instead it adopts an everyday, low-price strategy. The company does run folksy radio ads in local markets. In a current ad, Trader Joe's Chief Executive Officer Dan Bane pokes fun at other supermarkets that have installed flat-screen TVs for customers to watch at checkout counters. At Trader Joe's, he says, customers can entertain themselves by "actually talking" to employees.

Source: BusinessWeek, May 23, 2008

1. Chapter 23 identifies and defines three types of intensive growth strategy: market development, market penetration, and product development. In the spaces below, explain how Trader Joe's used each of these types of strategies in its growth. Provide specific examples in your explanation.

Market development

_____

_____

_____

Market penetration

_____

_____

_____

_____

_____

Product development

_____

_____

_____

_____

_____

2. Explain whether Trader Joe's uses vertical and horizontal integration in its growth. Provide specific examples in your explanation.

Vertical integration

_____

_____

_____

_____

Horizontal integration

_____

_____

_____

_____

3. How important has the development of personnel at Trader Joe's been to the success of the business?

_____

_____

_____

_____

_____

Chapter 23 Making Your Business Grow
Section 23.2 Challenges of Expansion
Section Review: Apply

Directions One type of growth funding is by public stock offering. When your company issues stocks or bonds, you must pay certain expenses. The amount that your business actually receives from the sale after paying these expenses is the net proceeds. Use this formula to answer the following questions:

Value of Issue − Total Selling Expenses = Net Proceeds

1. Pilgrim Utility Company issues 20,000 shares of stock at $35 per share.

Underwriting Expenses		Other Expenses	
Commissions	$42,000	Printing costs	$14,800
Legal fee	6,000	Legal fees	23,000
Advertising	4,700	Accounting fees	15,600
Miscellaneous	2,800	Miscellaneous	5,000

   What are the net proceeds after these selling expenses are deducted?

   _____

   _____

2. Global Corporation sold 400,000 shares of stock at $27.25 per share. The investment banker's commission was 6.3% of the value of the stock. The other expenses were 0.6% of the value of the stocks.
   What net proceeds did Global Corporation receive?

   _____

   _____

3. Riverside Development Co. sold 250,000 shares of stock at $28.75 per share. The underwriting commission was 5.4% of the value of the stocks. The other expenses were 0.9% of the value of the stocks.
   What net proceeds did Riverside Development receive?

   _____

   _____

Name _____ Date _____ Class _____

Chapter 23 Making Your Business Grow

Software Activity
Word Processing Application

Directions The objective of this activity is to write a promotion letter.

Practice Situation

You are the owner of a small accounting firm, Piedmont Accountants. Two other firms are located in your town—Titan Accountants and Joyner & Associates. The owner of Titan has decided to retire at the end of the year and has not found anyone interested in purchasing the firm.

You think that now would be an excellent time for you to expand your business by getting Titan clients to sign on with your firm. You have been doing business in your town for the past 15 years. You provide audit/accounting services, tax planning/preparation, business/personal financial planning, estate/retirement planning, business/asset valuation, and financial management.

You also believe that if you promote yourself to Titan clients, you should be successful in convincing many of them to sign on with your firm. You think that a good way to start is by writing a letter to Titan clients, where you could introduce yourself and encourage them to call for an appointment to discuss their future accounting needs.

Now, write a letter to these prospective clients. Your letterhead information has been completed for you and is shown below. If you wish to change that information, simply replace it with one of your own. Add the name of your city and state.

Piedmont Accountants

345 Professional Building
City, State, Zip Code

Today's Date

Word Processing Directions

1. Start your word processing software program.

2. Write your promotion letter. Type the letter in block style. Proofread and edit your work to make sure that it is correct and concise.

3. Save your work.

4. Print out a copy of your completed letter if your teacher has instructed you to do so.

5. Answer the following questions.

Interpreting Results

1. What should be your strongest argument for winning the business of these clients?

_____

_____

_____

_____

2. Why do entrepreneurs want their businesses to grow?

_____

_____

_____

_____

3. Other than trying to attract competitors' customers, what other strategies could entrepreneurs use to make their businesses grow?

_____

_____

_____

_____

Drawing Conclusions

4. What are some challenges you would face as you attempt to serve Titan clients?

_____

_____

_____

_____

Chapter 23 Making Your Business Grow
Academic Integration Activity

 English Language Arts
Recognizing Text Structure

Directions Read the following sentences. Circle the phrase that best describes the relationship represented in the sentences.

1. An entrepreneur puts together a good team and develops a practical concept. As a result, his or her new business probably will not stay small very long.

     sequence of events   cause and effect

2. Intensive growth strategies include market penetration, market development, and product development.

     statement and example   compare and contrast

3. Synergistic diversification involves finding new products or businesses that are compatible with your business. Conglomerate diversification involves finding products or businesses that are unrelated to your products or business.

     cause and effect   compare and contrast

4. With franchising, you personally train your franchisees. They, in turn, hire and are responsible for the employees who work for them.

     statement and example   compare and contrast

5. A shoe manufacturer eliminates intermediaries by selling directly to end users. Then, the manufacturer buys up the distributors and retailers of its shoes.

     cause and effect   sequence of events

6. With horizontal integration, you increase your market share and expand your business by buying up competitors. One such buyout was when Delta Air Lines bought Northwest Airlines and took over Northwest's old routes.

     statement and example   compare and contrast

7. Expansion creates challenges. Entrepreneurs must learn how to delegate managerial authority. Recordkeeping becomes more challenging.

     cause and effect   statement and example

8. Company A kept its business in private hands by seeking funding through venture capitalists. Company B raised funds through a public stock offering.

     cause and effect   compare and contrast

Chapter 23

Chapter 23 Making Your Business Grow

Academic Integration Activity

Social Studies
Initial Public Offering

Directions Read the article about Google's initial public offering (IPO), then answer the questions.

GOOGLE GOES PUBLIC

August 19, 2004, was one of the biggest days in the recent history of Wall Street. On that day, Google had its initial public offering (IPO), selling shares of stock to the public for the first time. On that day, approximately 1,000 Google employees became on-paper millionaires. Richest of all are founders Sergey Brin and Larry Page. According to recent figures, each owns Google stock worth at least $12 billion.

Google's original share price of $85 turned out to be quite a deal for those who bought stock on that August day. By 2007, shares were selling at more than $600. A stock market slump brought down Google's stock value; at the end of a recent trading session shares were still selling for $472.

The goal of the IPO, of course, was not only to make its founders and employees rich, but to raise money for company operations. What did Google do with this influx of cash? A lot of it has been used to acquire other companies. In 2004 Google bought Keyhole, Inc., which had a product called Earth Viewer. Google used the technology it acquired in the deal to launch Google Earth, a virtual globe, map, and geographic information program. In 2007 Google spent $3.1 billion to buy DoubleClick, a company that places advertisements on the Web. It paid $50 million for GrandCentral and turned it into Google Voice, an online telephone service. Google paid $625 million for Postini, an e-mail and Web security company.

Finally, the biggest deal of all: In 2006, for $1.65 billion in stock, Google became the owner of YouTube, one of the Internet's all-time most-visited sites.

---

1. A shareholder bought 100 shares of Google stock at the original share price. Calculate the amount paid for the stock (not including broker fees and other expenses).

   _____

2. The same shareholder later sold all 100 shares for $472 per share. Calculate the sale price and the profit the shareholder made (not including broker fees and other expenses).

   _____

3. In acquiring the other companies listed in the article, which integrative growth strategy did Google pursue?

   _____

4. Which diversification growth strategy did Google pursue?

   _____

Chapter 23 Making Your Business Grow
Case Study Activity
Nonprofit-Corporate Partnership

Directions Read the *BusinessWeek* Case Study feature in this chapter. Then read the information about Teach for America and use it to answer the questions that follow.

Partial List of Teach for America Employer Partnerships

Our country's top employers value the leadership skills and civic-minded nature that distinguish Teach for America alumni. Recognizing that corps members have gone through a highly selective process and have engaged in a challenging professional experience, our employer partners actively recruit our alumni for full-time positions and provide special benefits including two-year deferrals, career workshops, and professional mentoring.

Financial Services

Credit Suisse: Recruits college seniors, who have accepted their offer with Teach for America, and first year corps members for full-time positions in the Credit Suisse Investment Banking department to start after successful completion of the corps.

Deloitte: Two-year deferrals for students who receive job offers from specific businesses at Deloitte and are also accepted into Teach for America. Deloitte and Teach for America recruiters will have up-to-date information on which businesses are participating in the deferral program. Deloitte also recruits Teach for America corps members for full-time opportunities.

Law

Cadwalader, Wickersham & Taft LLP: Two-year deferrals for students who receive job offers from Cadwalader and are also accepted into Teach for America. Guaranteed call backs for qualified Teach for America alumni law students looking for full-time positions after graduation.

Continued on next page

Chapter 23 (side tab)

Management Consulting

Accenture: Two-year deferrals for students who receive job offers from Accenture's Management Consulting Strategy group and are also accepted into Teach for America. Accenture's Management Consulting Strategy group recruits Teach for America corps members for full-time opportunities.

Bain & Company: Two-year deferrals for students who receive job offers from Bain and are also accepted into Teach for America. Bain & Company recruits Teach for America corps members for full-time and summer internship opportunities.

Science and Technology

Google: Two-year deferrals for students who receive job offers from Google and are also accepted into Teach for America. Google mentors for corps members during their two year corps experience. Google will consider Teach for America corps members for full-time opportunities. (Google will treat Teach for America as a "core recruiting school.")

Excerpted from Teach for America's Web site

1. Describe a typical arrangement between Teach for America students and partner employees.

_____

_____

_____

2. Why do you think these employers work with Teach for America instead of competing with it? Explain.

_____

_____

_____

3. Why do you think Teach for America benefits from partnering with employers? Explain.

_____

_____

_____

Chapter 23 Making Your Business Grow

Test Prep
Sentence Completion

Directions Circle the letter of the word or phrase that best completes each of the following sentences.

1. Some factors that affect a company's ability to grow include _____.
   a. the characteristics of your target market
   b. how innovative your industry is
   c. your ability to get everyone to think entrepreneurially
   d. all of the above

2. Multiple sites for the business present all of the following challenges except _____.
   a. the ability to expand the customer base
   b. whether the store should operate independently or not
   c. more complicated record keeping
   d. the need to hire additional managerial staff

3. The problem with success is _____.
   a. it does not come often enough
   b. you can take it for granted
   c. you might have to start pulling money out of the business
   d. b and c

4. Which of the following is *not* true about raising money for growth?
   a. It takes more time than you think.
   b. With a good plan, the deal will always work out.
   c. It costs more than you think.
   d. You may have to buy out your relatives.

5. You can fund the growth of your business through _____.
   a. the cash flows of the business
   b. a private placement
   c. an employee stock ownership plan
   d. all of the above

6. Strategies involving growth within your industry, either horizontally or vertically, are _____.
   a. integrative growth strategies
   b. market penetration
   c. intensive growth strategies
   d. diversification

7. Increasing the number of customers by taking your product to new geographic locations is _____.
   a. diversification
   b. market development
   c. private placement
   d. market penetration

Chapter 23

Chapter 24 Social and Ethical Responsibility

 Note Taking

Directions As you read, write notes, facts, and main ideas in the note-taking column. Write key words and short phrases in the cues column. Then summarize the section in the summary box.

Cues	Note Taking
• philanthropy: making charitable donations to human welfare	**SOCIAL RESPONSIBILITY** • Entrepreneurs have historically made contributions to society.
• ethics: guidelines for human behavior	**ETHICAL RESPONSIBILITY** • Ethical behavior is conduct that adheres to the moral codes by which people live and do business.
	Summary

Chapter 24 Social and Ethical Responsibility

Section 24.1 Social Responsibility

Section Review: Identify

Directions Review the following case study. Then provide recommendations based on the questions that follow.

Lucretia Guzman, a gourmet entrepreneur, is preparing to market a new product. In the past, she has used molded plastics containing large amounts of fluorohydrocarbons as containers for her product. With the growing interest in environmental concerns, she is reconsidering her options. The fluorohydrocarbon containers have a negative environmental impact and add to the nonbiodegradable materials being placed in landfills. However, they are much less expensive than other types of packaging.

Lucretia has recently learned about a new type of packaging that would work for her new product. This packaging is made of recycled paper but costs 15 percent more than the molded plastic containers.

Lucretia has forged her business success by keeping costs to a minimum so she could market her products below that of her competitors. She has established a loyal customer base that continues to expect high-quality products at reasonable prices. In order to use the recycled paper containers, she would have to substantially reduce her profit margin or pass the added cost on to her customers. This, of course, would make her prices less competitive, and she may lose business to other producers.

Lucretia has always attempted to run her business in an ethical and responsible manner, but now she is faced with a dilemma. Can you help her decide what to do?

1. What are the ethical issues in this scenario?

_____

_____

_____

_____

_____

_____

_____

_____

_____

_____

Continued on next page

Chapter 24

2. If you were one of Lucretia Guzman's customers, how would you respond to her questions of pricing versus environmental responsibility?

_____

_____

_____

_____

_____

3. How would you advise her?

_____

_____

_____

_____

4. What would you do if you were one of her customers and she chose to raise her prices?

_____

_____

_____

_____

_____

5. How could Lucretia most effectively market this change? Give specific examples of appropriate strategies and activities.

_____

_____

_____

_____

_____

_____

_____

Chapter 24 Social and Ethical Responsibility
Section 24.2 Ethical Responsibility
Section Review: Explain

Directions Read the scenario, then answer the questions that follow.

Nick is an 18-year-old high school senior. He lives at home, and his sole source of income for the past year has been pet sitting and mowing lawns. In January, just after his birthday, he received an unsolicited credit card application from a new electronics store that is targeting young consumers in a special promotion. The business is trying to establish loyalty among young people as they enter the workforce. The letter stated that he was preapproved for a card with a $1,000 limit. All he had to do was fill out, sign, and return the credit application.

Four weeks later, Nick received a new credit card with a $1,000 limit. With this newfound purchasing power, he bought some new stereo components and a watch for his girlfriend. The total charges were over $900.

At the end of February, he received his first statement detailing purchases and the minimum amount now owed. He did not have enough money to pay the bill, so he just threw it away. This continued for three months until the store threatened legal action to force Nick to pay the bill.

1. How would you assess the ethical behavior of the business that granted credit to Nick? Explain.

_____

_____

_____

_____

_____

2. How would you assess the ethical behavior of Nick in this situation? Explain.

_____

_____

_____

_____

_____

_____

Continued on next page

Chapter 24

3. If you were the judge with this case before you, how would you rule in terms of who is responsible for payment? Explain.

_____

_____

_____

_____

_____

_____

4. Who bears the cost if Nick is relieved of the responsibility to pay for the merchandise? Explain.

_____

_____

_____

_____

_____

_____

_____

_____

5. If you were the owner of the electronics business, what are some other marketing strategies you might use to attract young customers?

_____

_____

_____

_____

_____

_____

_____

_____

Chapter 24 Social and Ethical Responsibility

Software Activity
Word Processing Application

Directions The objective of this activity is to write a business letter.

Practice Situation

You are the owner of a small sporting goods store that has just been open for six months. This is the first month that you have made a profit. You strongly feel that business owners should find ways to give back to the community.

Today, you received the letter shown below requesting that you donate $1,500 to sponsor a local youth baseball team. Although you would love to contribute, you feel that at the present time you will not be able to make this donation since profits are still so questionable.

Write a letter to the chamber of commerce representative informing them of your decision. The letter should also emphasize your strong feelings about the need for business owners to support community activities.

Anytown Chamber of Commerce
2000 Main Street
Any town, Any state 30000

Today's Date

Dear New Business Owner:

As a new and vital part of our business community, I'm sure you are aware of the importance of providing activities for young people. This year, I am responsible for generating funds that will allow the Chamber to be able to sponsor twelve youth baseball teams. We need your help!

It takes approximately $1,500 to sponsor each team. I hope you would consider providing a donation to sponsor one team. Each year, these youth teams provide outstanding programs for the youth in our community. In addition to recreation, they also provide team building and leadership opportunities.

Can we count on you for a sponsorship? If I can answer other questions, you can contact me at the address listed above or by calling 555-1234. I look forward to working with you on this valuable project for our community.

Sincerely,

John Anderson
Youth Programs

Continued on next page

Chapter 24

Word Processing Directions

1. Start your word processing software program.

2. Write your response to Mr. Anderson's letter. Type the letter in block style. Proofread and edit your work to make sure that it is correct and concise.

3. Save your work.

4. Print out a copy of your completed letter if your teacher has instructed you to do so.

5. Answer the following questions.

Interpreting Results

1. Why is it important for entrepreneurs to give back to the community?

_____

_____

_____

_____

2. Exchange your completed letter with a classmate. How does your version differ from your classmate's? Reread your own letter. How would you change it after reading your classmate's response letter?

_____

_____

_____

_____

Drawing Conclusions

3. If you do not have the funds to fulfill their request, what could you offer the chamber of commerce?

_____

_____

_____

_____

_____

_____

Chapter 24 Social and Ethical Responsibility
Academic Integration Activity

English Language Arts
Writing Skills

Directions Using the six basic values of personal character—trustworthiness, respect, responsibility, fairness, caring, citizenship—outline how you believe each value applies to you and how they would influence the way you run your business. You can give specific applications of each value, or describe one or more in a general sense.

_____

_____

_____

_____

_____

_____

_____

_____

_____

_____

_____

_____

_____

_____

_____

_____

_____

_____

_____

_____

_____

_____

_____

_____

_____

_____

Chapter 24

Name _____ Date _____ Class _____

Chapter 24 Social and Ethical Responsibility

Academic Integration Activity

Social Studies
Philanthropic Giving

Directions Study the graph measuring total philanthropic giving in the United States. Then answer the questions.

TOTAL PHILANTHROPIC GIVING IN THE UNITED STATES

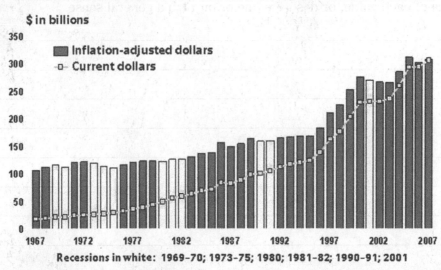

Recessions in white: 1969–70; 1973–75; 1980; 1981–82; 1990–91; 2001

Source: Grenzebach Glier and Associates

1. In inflation-adjusted dollars, what was the approximate total philanthropic giving amount in 1967?

   _____

2. What was the total approximate amount in 2007?

   _____

3. Which five-year period had the biggest increase in philanthropic giving?

   _____

4. In which year was the largest amount given?

   _____

5. What could be inferred from the showing of periods of economic recession (negative growth) in the graph?

   _____

   _____

   _____

Chapter 24 Social and Ethical Responsibility

Case Study Activity

Social Entrepreneurship

Directions Read the *BusinessWeek* Case Study feature in this chapter. Then read the information about *BusinessWeek's* "Most Promising Social Entrepreneurs" and use it to complete the Case Study Activity.

BusinessWeek magazine's *SmallBiz* team recently asked readers to help track down trailblazing American companies, in operation at least a year, which aimed to turn a profit while tackling societal problems. Readers selected the following five companies as the U.S.'s Most Promising Social Entrepreneurs:

#1: Better World Books—Online book seller

#2: Impact Makers—Health-care management and consulting company

#3: Stonyfield Farm—Organic yogurt maker

#4: Academic Earth—University lecture video Web site

#5: CleanFish—Company that helps small-scale fishers bring sustainable fish to restaurants and market

Select one of these companies for an Internet research activity. Use search engines and the company's Web site to find the following information about the selected company.

_____

1. Name of company and headquarters

_____

2. Company founder(s) and year founded

_____

3. Number of employees

_____

4. Description of main socially-responsible activities

_____

5. Most recently available annual revenues

_____

Chapter 24

Chapter 24 Social and Ethical Responsibility

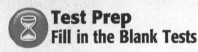

Test Prep
Fill in the Blank Tests

Directions Take the practice test below. Complete the sentences with content vocabulary and terms from the word bank.

infringement	Truth-in-Lending Act	international markets	philanthropy
bribes	social responsibility	Fair Credit Billing Act	conflict of interest
values	customer service	ethics	

1. Regulations govern how a business can treat its customers, but most businesses consider _____ their most important competitive advantage.

2. It is easier to make decisions when you do not consider actions that go against your _____.

3. _____ mean(s) that a business acknowledges that it has a contract with society.

4. Your _____ is/are your guidelines for your behavior and is/are based on your values.

5. The _____ specify(ies) how quickly businesses must respond to consumer complaints.

6. _____ present(s) some especially challenging ethical dilemmas for American businesses.

7. The _____ ensure(s) that businesses fully inform customers about purchases.

8. A multimillionaire's $100,000 donation to help fund the building of a new community center is an act of _____.

9. Illegal payments made to secure special services for a business are called _____.

10. A _____ is a clash between a person's private interests and his/her responsibilities as a person in a position of trust.

11. Copyright _____ is unethical and not respectful of the person or business that owns the patent or copyright.